How to Live
with Parents and Teachers

How to Live with Parents and Teachers

Eric W. Johnson

The Westminster Press
Philadelphia

© 1986 Eric W. Johnson

All rights reserved—no part of this book may be reproduced in any form without permission in writing from the publisher, except by a reviewer who wishes to quote brief passages in connection with a review in magazine or newspaper.

Book design by Gene Harris

First edition

Published by The Westminster Press®
Philadelphia, Pennsylvania

PRINTED IN THE UNITED STATES OF AMERICA
9 8 7 6 5 4 3 2 1

Library of Congress Cataloging-in-Publication Data

Johnson, Eric W.
  How to live with parents and teachers.

  Bibliography: p.
  Includes indexes.
  SUMMARY: One hundred short bits of advice, arranged in alphabetical order, to help teenagers get along with parents and teachers, under topical headings such as alcohol, anger, chores, grades, guilt, money, teasing, unfairness, and yelling.
  1. Youth—United States—Life skills guides—Juvenile literature. 2. Youth—United States—Family relationships—Juvenile literature. 3. Teacher-student relationships—United States—Juvenile literature.
  [1. Parent and child. 2. Teacher-student relationships]
  I. Title.
HQ796.J5716 1986   305.2′35′0973   86-9273

ISBN 0-664-22184-X (pbk)

Contents

What's in This Book for You? ...7

Adolescence ...15
Alcohol ...16
Allowances ...19
Anger ...19
Appearance ...21
Arguments ...23
Blaming ...25
Body language ...26
Boredom ...27
Cheating ...28
Child abuse ...29
Chores ...30
Communication ...32
Competition ...33
Conflicts ...34
Criticism ...36
Cursing ...38
Dating ...38
Death ...40
Discipline ...41
Divorce ...42
Drugs ...46
Embarrassment ...47

Feelings ...48
Fights ...51
Free time ...51
Friends ...52
Generation gap ...55
Goals ...55
Grades ...57
Grandparents ...58
Guilt ...59
Hating ...60
Health ...61
Help ...62
Honesty ...64
Hours ...65
Humor ...66
Ideals ...67
Incest ...68
Jobs ...69
Language ...71
Listening ...72
Love ...74
Manners ...76
Mistakes ...78
Money ...79
Moods ...81

Music	82	Selfishness	116
Negotiating	83	Sex	118
Normalcy	84	Sex roles	122
Openness	85	Smoking	125
Orders	87	Standards	126
Parent-teacher conferences	88	Study habits	127
		Suicide	130
Parties	89	Talking things over	131
Peer pressure	92	Teacher's pet	133
Pets	94	Teasing	135
Please and thanks	94	Telephone	135
Popularity	94	Tests	137
Praise	96	Time together	140
Problem-solving	97	Tone of voice	141
Promises	99	Transportation	142
Protesting	100	TV	143
Punishment	100	Unfairness	146
Put-downs	102	Values	147
Questioning	102	Words	148
Reading	103	Work load	149
Rebellion	104	Yelling	149
Religion	105	Your room/locker/desk	150
Report cards	105		
Reputation	106	You yourself	151
Responsibility	107	Bibliography	153
Rewards	109		
Rights	109	Index of Games and Activities	154
Rules	110		
Running away	113		
Secrets	114	Index of Subjects	155

What's in This Book for You?

This book is addressed to teenagers. Its purpose is to give you help when you need it, or even before you need it, in how to get along—to live—with your parents and teachers. The book is long on practical suggestions, short on theory. The practical suggestions come in a hundred short bits arranged in alphabetical order. They range from **adolescence, alcohol,** and **anger** through **death, divorce,** and **drugs**; from **rebellion, religion,** and **report cards** down to **your room** and **you yourself**. There's a complete list in the contents.

Most teenagers usually do pretty well in getting along with their parents and teachers. However, many of you sometimes find it tough going, and quite a few of you find it tough going a lot of the time. Whatever your own situation may be, there are probably times when you wish things could be better—when you could use some help. At least that's what teenagers tell me.

Your parents and teachers probably could use some help too, in learning how to live with *you*, even though they may not feel like admitting it. You might even want to get a copy of this book and give it to your parents or some teachers for a birthday or Christmas present. If you do, you'd better read it first. Then, if you give it, don't do it with a note saying, "Here's a book you really *need*. Enjoy it!" Better, maybe, to say, "Here's a book you might enjoy. When you've read it, how about if we discuss it?"

Something We All Have in Common
There's one basic thing all teenagers, parents, and teachers have in common: We are human beings. We all

What's in This Book for You? 8

act like human beings. Yes, we do, even when we act objectionably. And since we are all human beings, we have the possibility of living well together.

All human beings, by the time they are your age, also have in common certain needs. I have written down what I think these needs are. Before you read my list, it might be interesting for you to try making your own. Then compare your list with mine. As you read each item, ask yourself, "Do I need this? Do my parents? Do my teachers?"

First, seven utterly basic needs:

- food
- shelter (house, apartment)
- clothing
- sleep
- love (a feeling of closeness to one or more persons)
- self-respect
- the respect of others

Next, thirty other very important needs:

- advice (not too much)
- to blow off steam
- challenge (not too much)
- change (not too much)
- criticism (in small amounts)
- to deal with conflict
- education (including how to speak, read, write, and figure; facts about how people work; facts about how the world works)
- to express ourselves
- freedom (not too much)
- friends
- fun
- health care
- to hear (listen)
- to be heard (listened to)
- help (not too much)
- honesty (truthfulness)
- humor (and to laugh)

- independence (not too much)
- knowledge
- limits (some order; set by ourselves, set by others)
- money (some)
- pleasure (bodily, emotional, mental)
- praise
- privacy
- to question (ask questions, express doubts)
- safety (not total)
- sharing (of feelings, ideas, things)
- to speak
- sympathy (a deep sort of sharing)
- work (useful work)

Again: do you need all those? Do your parents? Do your teachers?

You Are Unique—One of a Kind

These needs are what people of all ages have in common. Don't forget, however, that each person in the world is unique. You are unique. Unless you are an identical twin, you are genetically unique. That is, from the moment your father's sperm joined your mother's ovum (egg), you had your own unique heredity. You began as a combination of microscopically small structures called *genes*, from both your mother and father. And no two people in the world (except for identical twins) have the same combination of genes. Members of families may look alike, or people may say you inherit this from your mother or that from your father, but mainly you are you and nobody else, both on the surface and inside your body.

Even if you are an identical twin (or triplet, or whatever), you are still unique, because from the moment you were born, the outside world, your environment, began to influence you. No two people, even in the closest of families, are treated exactly the same. And they are treated even more differently outside the family. So the equation for you, and every other human being, might be written:

Your unique heredity + your unique environment = unique you, or YUH + YUE = UY

Common Needs Can Cause Conflict and Competition

Let's go back to the idea that as human beings we all have somewhat the same needs. Needing the same sorts of things means more than just giving teenagers, parents, and teachers the possibility of working well together and understanding each other. Common needs can also result in conflict and competition, because often we each want more of whatever it may be than is easily available, and so we may compete for it. One obvious example is money. Other examples are our needs for freedom or fun, say, or for privacy or sympathy or understanding. Our needs may get in the way of other people who are trying to provide for their needs for the same things. Or our need to feel important and respected may be seen as interfering with another's need to feel important and respected. Of course, all this is true not just between teenagers and their parents and teachers but also between teenagers themselves. That's why "to deal with conflict" is a basic human need no matter how old we are.

How to Read This Book

When I told one of my daughters about the title, she said, "Why not call it 'How to Live *Without* Parents and Teachers'?" She made a good point. Your ultimate aim is to grow up, become independent, and be your own person, standing on your own two feet and not leaning on parents and teachers, even though you may still enjoy them as people. But teenagers, on the whole, are not old enough yet to be completely independent.

Meanwhile, I've tried to make this book both practical and easy to use. There are a great many specific suggestions and ideas you may want to try out, in order to get along better with your parents and teachers. In some of the topics I suggest games or specific activities, set apart so you can find them easily. And they are listed in an index. These games and activities are useful, and often fun, as you and your parents and teachers go about the business of living together. When a word in the middle of a sentence is printed in **blacker type**, like that, it's a signal that you'll find a related topic by that title in its alphabetical place in the book.

Probably you'll want to refer to certain topics when they come up in your own life, rather than read straight through from A to Z. On the other hand, if you do go through in order (maybe skipping parts that don't seem useful at the moment), you'll have gotten a lot of ideas you can go back to when you need them. You also might mark certain ones you'd like to share with your parents or teachers when the time is right.

"Who are you, Eric Johnson, to tell me what to do?"

If you are asking this question, good for you. Why should you read a book covering so many kinds of subjects unless there's some possibility that the author knows what he's talking about? Well, I admit right off that the amount I don't know is much larger than the amount I do know. I agree, too, with whoever it was who said, "Education is going from cocksure ignorance to thoughtful uncertainty." I'm thoughtfully uncertain about quite a few of these topics. But I have written what my reading, writing, teaching, parenting, and living have taught me.

I was a teacher of boys and girls in grades 4 through 12, but mostly grades 7 and 8, for twenty-six years. I've taught English, history, social studies, and sex education in both public and private schools. I've written about thirty books, several *about* teenagers or written *for* teenagers. (Some of them are listed in the Bibliography at the back of the book.)

Further, over the years I've visited about 150 schools, parents' groups, students' groups, parent-teacher associations, and teachers' conferences, discussing and working on the topics I write about here. I've learned a lot from these visits. And I have three former teenagers of my own, not to mention a very wise and understanding wife.

As I watch papers, magazines, and stores for books

What's in This Book for You?

about family and school relationships, I am constantly surprised by how many more books there are on how to get along with you teenagers than there are on how *you* can manage to live with us parents and teachers. And often the books are written as if *you* were the main problem. Take the title *Help! I've Got a Teenager.* If I were a teen, I'd feel like saying, "Help! Help! I've got parents *and* a lot of teachers!"

Be that as it may, here are three suggestions for you. Each is both general and specific.

1. Be polite when it doesn't go against your principles. Both parents and teachers are delighted by a spontaneous, unasked-for, enthusiastic thank-you: "Gee, thanks, I really liked that!" Another kind of politeness is the offer of help beyond arranged duties and chores: "Let me unload the groceries"; "I'll finish the vacuuming"; "I'll erase the board"; "We'll put those books back."

2. Acknowledge that your parents and teachers are right when you really think they are. This does not mean being an apple-polisher or a yes-person. It means that if you see people are right, even if you opposed them, you simply say so. It gives people great satisfaction, it makes them feel good, and it removes the necessity for them to keep insisting that they are right or to use that revolting expression, "I told you so." If you admit they are right, they don't have to prove it. It also puts you in a much stronger position another time, when you're sure that *you* are right. You can say so, and you will be listened to with respect.

3. Take the lead, when you can, in talking, opening up, expressing your feelings, keeping your parents up-to-date in your life and informed about how things are with you. Nothing is more rewarding and satisfying to parents or teachers than to feel that their sons and daughters, or their students, are trying to keep the flow of communication open.

It's not always easy to get along with people—parents, teachers, *or* teenagers. It's amazing how well we do much of the time, despite the fact that we are all such complex human beings. Do your best, give it a good try, *keep* trying, but don't expect to be perfect. It's not human nature to be perfect, and you are human. And don't be put off if you sometimes get some put-downs, like the girl who said to her mother, "But, Mom, I'm *trying!*" and her mother answered, "I know you are, dear, *very* trying."

Consideration of the feelings and situations of others is perhaps the most important attitude for people to have if they want to live well together. And consideration requires imagination. You've got to be able to imagine yourself in the other person's place. As the French say, "Put yourself in the other person's skin."

That's not easy to do, as is illustrated by a true story about two small children, Julie, eight, and her brother Michael, five. They were riding escalators in the Neiman-Marcus department store in Dallas, Texas, while their parents were shopping. It was a hot day, and they each had a large ice-cream cone. On the way up one escalator, all crowded together, Julie was standing behind Michael, and Michael was standing behind a woman wearing a beautiful mink coat. Julie looked at Michael in horror. His dripping cone was pressed against the mink. "Watch out, Michael!" she whispered. "You're getting fur all over your ice cream!"

Well, if you are to live well with parents and teachers, you'll have to learn to put yourself in their shoes—and in their coats.

adolescence

For many young people, the period called adolescence is one during which it is especially difficult to live comfortably with parents and teachers. By adolescence we mean the period between puberty and adulthood, during which people grow from children into adults. For a girl, puberty begins when she first menstruates; for a boy, when he first ejaculates semen. A girl has now reached the time when she can become pregnant; a boy can now make a girl or woman pregnant. (Our word *adolescence* comes from the Latin word *adolescere*, "to grow up.")

Adolescence is a most remarkable time of life, when a person experiences all sorts of new **feelings** of body and mind, many of them having to do with **sex**. These feelings can be exciting, disturbing, enjoyable, frustrating, and puzzling—to you, to parents, to teachers. When you are going through adolescence, you may sometimes be very difficult to live with because you tend to be wrapped up in your own development. Your mind also becomes more complex and interesting, full of new ideas and with a greater desire for independence. Adolescence has been described as "like a house on moving day—a temporary mess."

If you are going to manage to live well with parents and teachers during adolescence, it's a good idea to keep these considerations in mind. Remember that you may be difficult and try to allow for it. Know, too, that many parents and teachers expect you to be difficult. They may even use **put-downs**: "That adolescent!" Many parents are surprised and shocked by the way their children are developing. Teachers will be less surprised because they are used to teaching adolescents and know what to expect.

But adolescence is a marvelous time of life. Furthermore, it is inevitable. You are bound to grow from childhood to adulthood. As you do, you tend to depend less and less on your parents and teachers and more on your peers— people your own age. This is a good part of growing up, but it can be especially hard on parents. Many parents find it difficult to give up the easier relationships of childhood. Keep this in mind if you want to live well with them.

One advantage of adolescence is that your mind is developing fast and becoming mature enough to enable you to stand back and look at yourself and how you are behaving. You can also look at your parents and teachers more objectively, as individual human beings rather than accepted figures of authority. So, when you can, do use your mind to observe and study your own acts and feelings, and those of your parents and teachers. This will help you see how what you say and do affects others, and seeing this helps you live better with them.

advice see help

alcohol

In many families, alcohol is a major cause of conflict and friction. Let's start with a few facts. Alcohol is a drug, the most abused drug there is in the U.S.A. Alcohol is contained in drinks like wine, beer, ale, whiskey, gin, vodka, and brandy. Drinking alcoholic beverages is a great pleasure for many people and is very much a part of our culture. When people drink, the alcohol often gives them pleasant feelings of relaxation and friendliness toward others. But if people drink too much, they become intoxicated (drunk) and lose control of themselves in different ways. Some become very talkative; some lose judgment and get into fights, even dangerous ones; others become very sleepy and zonk out; still others lose judgment about **sex** and may have sexual intercourse without really knowing what they are doing or remembering what the consequences may be. People who drive cars while under the influence of alcohol are much more likely to have accidents. Drunken driving is against the law.

People can become addicted to alcohol. Such people—*alcoholics*—are unable to resist drinking too much. Alcohol addiction has ruined millions of lives in our country. The only way for an alcoholic to recover from addiction is to stop drinking entirely. Really heavy drinking, especially if done in combination with other drugs, can kill you.

In most states it is illegal to sell or serve alcohol to

people under the age of 18 or 21. The assumption is that people under the legal drinking age do not have the judgment and maturity to manage the effects of alcohol.

Given these facts, you can understand why most parents are concerned and frightened if they know or suspect that their children are drinking, even if only now and then at parties. The best way to live well with your parents as far as drinking goes is to make up your mind not to drink at all, to tell them that this is your policy, and to stick to it. But it is probably much easier for me to say this than for you to do it, because of the pressures you may feel from your friends and because you may really want to try what is for so many people a pleasurable part of life.

Also, drinking may be a regular part of your parents' lives. If your father or mother comes home after a rough day at work and says something like "Boy, what a day! I'm ready for a drink!" it's easy for you to feel the same way when you have had a hard day. Also, when you see your or other people's parents having a good time drinking with friends, it can put pressure on you to want to try it.

If alcohol and what to do about it are a problem in your family, or even if there's no problem but just interest, find some relaxed times when you can talk over the whole subject with them. Among other things, you might discuss what they think and do about drinking and why; what your feelings are about their drinking and the possibility of your drinking; what your friends do about drinking. This does not mean that you should expect your parents' behavior to be like yours or yours like theirs. After all, they are adults; you are a teenager on the way to adulthood. But the discussion will help you meet the pressures in your life and will help your parents understand the situations you are in and the decisions you may have to make.

In many houses, there's a closet or cupboard where the liquor bottles are kept. If you feel like sneaking a drink when your parents are out, *don't!* Tell your parents how you feel, even though they might get angry at you for even feeling that way. It's better for life at home to have things out in the open.

Another matter is **parties**, those you may go to or that you may have at your house. Never, but never, sneak a few beers or a bottle of something to a party. It's a likely way to get into trouble, and it's unfair to the parents and kids at whose house the party takes place, as well as to the kids who go. If you find that others have sneaked drinks, don't have any part of it, and as soon as you can, let your parents know so they can plan with you what to do so that such situations don't arise again. If someone sneaks drinks to your house, or just outside your house while there's a party inside, either deal with it yourself, promptly and frankly, or explain to your parents and ask your parents to deal with it. Try to work out an understanding with them ahead of time.

An especially difficult situation is when parents abuse alcohol and can't stop. Alcoholic parents are a terrible problem, both for themselves and for their families. Some parents may be unaware of how hard they are making life for their families. Often they do not even admit that they are alcoholics. It's really important to let them know. If you can do this without getting angry or acting disgusted or hateful, you have a better chance of helping an alcoholic parent. Tell parents how their drinking makes you feel. If you don't, they may not know. And always remember that if your parents abuse alcohol, it's not *your* fault. Alcoholism is a sickness, too complex for you to deal with. Therefore, it's best to get help. After you let both your parents know how you feel, probably the next step is to talk to someone else: a trusted relative, a counselor, your pastor, a teacher, or a friend of the family in whom you have confidence. There are organizations, like Alcoholics Anonymous, which are very successful in helping alcoholics who want to solve their problems. A related organization is Alateen, which helps teenagers whose parents are alcoholics. Write to Al-Anon Family Group Headquarters, One Park Avenue, New York, NY 10016, or phone 212-683-1771, for information and meeting times of a group in your area.

allowances

Teenagers, and most other people too, need some money to spend as they want without accounting for it. Some children have jobs. But most families provide their children from a quite early age with an allowance of money to meet this need. How large should the allowance be? Should you have to do certain chores to earn it? If you disobey some rules your family has set up, or if you misbehave in some way, should you have to take a cut in your allowance as your punishment?

The best way to answer these questions is to talk them over and agree on a policy. My feeling is that, for most families, chores and allowances should be separate from each other, with an agreed-upon policy for each one. Nor do I think misbehavior should be punished by a cut in allowance. An allowance meets genuine needs that don't go away, and it doesn't seem helpful, for teenagers growing to adulthood, to have to come and ask Mom or Dad for money whenever they need some.

But these are only my opinions. Families work well under many different plans. Your family will have to work out its own.

anger

Anger is a natural part of human behavior. As you know, parents get angry, teachers get angry, your friends get angry, you get angry. Anger is one means of communication. If a person gets angry, or looks angry, it's a way of saying "Watch out! I feel strongly about this," or "I'm in a bad mood right now so treat me carefully," or even "This is something that frightens me!" It helps you to get along well with parents and teachers if you know what makes them angry or can tell when they seem close to anger. It's helpful to them to know the same things about you. Don't hesitate to say, in a calm moment, "You know what really makes me angry? It's when . . . "

So: it's all right to get angry sometimes and to express your anger. But, if you are to live well with people, don't express anger by hitting. Also, when you're angry, you may say things you feel at the moment of anger but don't really feel most of the time, like "I could kill you!" or "I hate you!" (See **yelling**.) Therefore, when the moment of anger passes, try to find a time to *explain* why you were angry and to say in some way, "Really, I love you." Anger does not mean the end of love. In fact, couples who say "We've been married for thirty years and have never had a cross word" are probably either so scared of their deep anger they don't dare express it or they aren't telling the truth.

There are days for many of us when *everybody* seems to be doing things wrong and making us annoyed or angry. If you're having one of those days, you can be pretty sure it isn't the whole world that's wrong, it's you. So it's a good idea to be extra careful and ask, "What's wrong with me today that makes everybody seem wrong?" It may even make you have a friendly laugh at yourself.

Handling anger at home. If possible, be angry at the situation or the action, not the person who caused it. "I *hate* it when you mess around with things in my room!" or "Boy, I really get mad when you bug me about my homework!" You "hate" what's done, not the person who does it. "Hate the sin, not the sinner." If you feel terribly angry, go run around the block a few times, preferably without slamming the door as you go out. If a parent is angry at you, listen and then say softly, "OK, I think I understand. What makes you mad is when I . . . " Then talk about it. If your family just can't take it when people express their anger, find a friendly adult you have confidence in and talk about it.

"What Makes Me Angry"

When you are angry but know that expressing your anger is going to make things worse, go to your room and write down what's making you angry. If, after an hour or so, it still seems worth it, show your parents what you wrote. If there are a lot of angry feelings in your house, suggest that everybody write about "What makes me angry" or "The last two times I felt angry in this house." Then share what you all wrote. It will help you all to understand each other better, and it may even get a few laughs.

Handling anger at school. Try to remember that teachers have a lot of students to teach. They also are supposed to "keep order." For most of them, it's very hard now and then to avoid getting angry and saying so, maybe loudly. The best way to get along with an angry teacher is to listen, try to figure out what you can do to make things better, and, above all, not get angry back.

Try as hard as you can *never* to show in a loud or conspicuous way in class that you are mad at a teacher. Student anger is very hard for most teachers; it seems to challenge the authority and control they must exercise. So hold your peace and ask (maybe by writing a polite note) if you can't talk over the problem.

If you're given an assignment to write on whatever you choose to, write a careful paper on "What Makes Me Angry at School" or even ask the teacher to assign such a topic.

Remember that some teachers, often for very good reason, *act* angry just to get results. The device works quite well if not used too often. So observe the "anger" and stop doing anything you shouldn't do. A useful tool for some teachers is to have what the writer P. G. Wodehouse called "an eye that could open an oyster at twenty paces." Respect such an eye—and hope, too, for a smile or word that can open a heart at twenty paces.

appearance

How you look says a lot to people, and says it quickly. Your parents know this, and therefore your appearance is important to them. (Obviously, too, how *they* look is important to you.) Differences in opinion about appearance, both what people look like and how they are dressed, can cause difficulties in getting along together. Your appearance sends out messages to others.

Also one not-so-simple fact is that how people think they look affects how well they can live with others. If you think you look ugly or strange, it tends to make you feel bad *appearance* 22

about yourself, and that can make you irritable and hard to live with. If you think you look OK, it is likely to make you easier to live with. An important and comforting thing to remember is that there is no one single way everybody should look, even though TV and newspaper ads may try to make us think there is. Keep in mind how many different-looking people are friends, fall in love, are happily married, live well together. Remember, too, that how you look is less important than what you are and how you act toward people.

It can help a lot to ask now and then, "Do I look OK, Mom?" or "Dad, how do you like this T-shirt?" Or ask about hair or makeup. You can listen and take what you hear into account, even though *you* are the main one to decide what you'll look like, or at least what you'll do with the basic looks you've got. It's also important to explain to parents how your friends feel about how you look. Sometimes it will help if you remind your parents that your world, like theirs, has at least three parts in it—home, school, friends—and you have to live in all three. Within limits, you have a right to assert your freedom of appearance. The limits are set by what sends out a message that is acceptable to your parents and to your school.

Two other parts of appearance are posture—how you stand and sit—and **manners**, particularly table manners. Try to keep aware of how your parents feel about these. A slouchy, sloppy kid can seem an insult to a family, and people don't like to be insulted.

What about teachers at school? First of all, don't forget teachers have to look at you, just as much as you have to look at them. It helps them feel good about you if they like what they see: the appearance of attention, interest, respect, neatness. If there are regulations about clothing, follow them as carefully as you can. If there are no regulations, dress in a way that is appropriate to a classroom. This probably means not being conspicuous if it seems to distract classmates or teachers. If you want to live well with teachers, don't use school as a place to show off weird clothes or hairstyles.

One other point about appearance. Often, whether it should or not, if your homework and papers look neat it makes life easier for teachers. Don't spend a long time making perfect copies of everything you hand in; that's wasteful. But let your work give the appearance of having been done by a person who cares.

Note: The teenage years are a time when some people have extra troubles with their complexion—pimples and acne. If you feel that your face looks terrible because of acne, you may become shy or irritable and feel bad about yourself. First, be assured that acne and pimples are almost always much more noticeable to the person who sees them in the mirror than they are to anybody else. Don't let feeling bad about your skin make you hard to live with—but if you think your condition is serious, talk with your parents or with the school nurse, or your doctor, or a dermatologist.

arguments

Arguments are a normal part of living with people, a normal kind of communication. Often, if they are not too heated and angry, they are very helpful because they reveal people's feelings as well as their ideas, and if you want to live well with parents and teachers, and they with you, it's good to know what you all feel and think.

Also, arguments are a method of reaching agreement on problems of living together, problems about what to do or who is to do what and problems about what people think. As you know, lawyers "argue" a case. That is, they think up all the reasons they can to prove something to convince a judge or a jury. Of course, lawyers argue to win, whereas with arguments at home and school it's much better to argue simply to solve a problem and enjoy the result.

Keep in mind that a vigorous argument doesn't mean the end of love. If your parents argue, even loudly, and even if they express a lot of anger, it doesn't mean they don't love each other. It would be scarier if they were afraid to argue.

Arguing with parents. To argue well with parents, try

arguments 24

to enjoy the argument. Laugh at the funny things that are said (but never at the person who says them). Smile now and then to show that basically things are still all right. Don't walk out of an argument angrily. If it's too much for you, say, "Let's talk about this later when I've had a chance to calm down."

Try to find an answer, not to win a victory; search for truth, even a small truth. If you find you've reached an agreement, say something like, "OK, do we agree? We'll ..." whatever you've agreed to. But remember that often an argument doesn't end in an agreement. At least, if people listen in an argument, they learn more about the other people, and that's a big help in getting along. In almost every case, since it's your parents' house and they are the adults and the ones responsible, if you can't agree, you'd better go along with them. You can always bring up the discussion again later.

Argue the Other Side

Sometimes it's useful—and fun—to reverse roles. Pretend you're a parent and argue from the parent's point of view, and let your parents try to argue your point of view.

Arguing with teachers. Teachers are expected to keep order in a classroom, so you have to be especially careful about arguing with them. They need, if a crisis arises, to be able to "control the class." (This doesn't mean they should control your mind or feelings. Nobody can do that!) But some teachers like to argue with their classes, and to have different students argue with each other. As a part of their teaching, they will make a certain statement just to get a good discussion, or argument, going.

If in doubt about arguing with teachers, don't. Instead, raise a question for discussion.

Put up your hand and be recognized before you speak. If the subject of the argument is at all personal, find a time after class to argue it.

Don't challenge a teacher's authority or control of the

class. If you're sure the teacher is wrong about a matter of fact or the answer to a problem, don't say, "You're wrong"—unless you're sure the teacher likes you to do that. Instead, raise the question and state some evidence or refer to something in a book—maybe the next day, or after class.

blaming

If you do something wrong, nothing is more tempting than to blame someone else. You want to stay out of trouble, so you say, "*He* did it!" or "*She* did it! *I* didn't do it!" And just as you may blame others, so others may blame you. Nothing is more tempting than blaming, and few things are more harmful.

So what if someone has done something wrong? If it was you who did it, the best policy is to be courageous and admit it. Accept the blame and admit what you've done. There are several advantages to doing this. Parents and teachers (and your friends, too) will admire you for it. Also, it's the truth and so helps clear the air, and it's easier to live together in clear air than in air murky with faultfinding. Plus, it will make it easier later for others to admit when they've done something wrong. And if, as you accept the blame, you can honestly say "I'm sorry," it makes other people feel good about you, and people who feel good about you are easier to live with.

There may be strong reasons why you did what you did, even if it turned out to be wrong. If so, don't hesitate to explain, but just give the facts. However, if you are blamed for doing something you didn't do, stick up for yourself. Instead of simply saying, "I did not!" say calmly (calmness often disarms people), "I didn't do it; what makes you think I did?" Stick to the evidence. Accepting blame for something you didn't do doesn't help anybody. In fact, it weakens the person who actually did do it.

If you know someone else is at fault, even your parents or a teacher, be careful how you go about blaming. Describe the facts. Put the blame as a question rather than a statement: "Did you leave the refrigerator door open?"

"Did you forget to pass out that homework assignment?" Never say, "You *always* . . . " whatever it is. That's tough to live with. Stick to the situation now; never mind yesterday or tomorrow. And respect excuses if they are genuine.

How about school? If you know who it was who did something that was harmful or against the rules, should you tell the teacher or principal? I think you should, with care and after talking with the person who did it. Why? See **honesty**.

body language

Often you can tell how people feel from the way their faces and bodies look. This is called *body language*. If your father comes home slumped over and moving slowly, if he sits with his head down, or if his arms hang loosely, or if he has a grim expression on his face, all this may be saying, "I've had a hard day" or "I feel discouraged" or "The whole world seems to be against me." If your mother moves rapidly about the house, smiles cheerfully but says nothing, and then plumps down in the kitchen, suddenly relaxed, to drink a cup of coffee, her body actions at first probably were saying, "Don't get in my way. This is no time to talk." A few minutes later, in the kitchen, her body may be saying, "I feel good. I've gotten a good job done."

You may be able to tell how your teachers are feeling by the way they sit, stand, write on the chalkboard, or move about the room, as well as by their facial expressions. Clenched hands, tapping feet, looking away from people rather than right at them—all these are ways the body talks. If you take a moment to "read" the bodies of your parents and teachers, you may get useful messages. And they can read messages from your body, too. *See also* **language**.

Pantomimes

A pantomime is an interesting way to use body language to get across ideas: you act out an event or series of events using no words, only your body and facial expressions. Lightened with humor, it is a nonthreatening way to put across feelings and ideas about the problems of living together, either at home or at school.

Do as the world's best-known mime, Marcel Marceau, does before each pantomime: give its title, so that people spend their time watching you, not just guessing. Some titles you might use are: "Coming Home After Work"; "Off to School"; "What Program Shall We Watch?"; "How X Acts in an Argument"; "Telephone Problems"; "Dad Meets My New Friend"; "Cleaning My Room"; "The Adventures of a Gum Chewer"; "How to Get a Bad Reputation." You'll think of many others. Pantomimes are a great way to send messages without threats, and they often lead to good discussions afterward.

books *see* reading

boredom

"This is *so* boring!" If you want to get along well with your teachers, never say that. It may be true, but your teachers have probably prepared their lessons carefully, believe that the lessons are important, and have tried their best to make them interesting. When teachers have done that and then hear "Bor-*ing!*" they're likely to be insulted or discouraged and to resent the student who makes such a remark.

So what should you do if the work does indeed bore you? Sometimes it's best just to do it with the appearance of cheerfulness. Then have something really interesting to do afterward, like a good book to read or some problems to solve. Or ask yourself, "Why is this important to do?" If you can figure out why, it may make the assignment less tedious.

If you can't discover any importance in the work (except keeping out of trouble), find a time in private to ask the teacher to explain its value. When you've finished, you could write at the bottom of your paper your questions about it and suggest tactfully, if you can, some interesting work that might teach the needed material or skills. And if the lesson is something you've mastered already, ask your teacher if you can take a test on it and then be allowed to do some advanced work, for extra credit, or go ahead quietly on a project of your own.

However, face the fact that you do have to learn to live through some boredom. However, also, most teachers will be grateful to hear if some of the lessons they are assigning are, in fact, seen by their pupils as dull or pointless. So don't just live in dull boredom. Find a way to discuss it.

the car see transportation

cheating

In the long run, a person who cheats is never as easy to live with as an honest person. So don't cheat; be honest.

Of course, that's easy to say but not so easy to do. Why do people cheat? It's not always simple. Maybe they don't understand the importance of being honest. They are scared of the consequences of honesty—like doing poorly on a test or being punished for poor performance. Or they very much want to do well and can't. (This may cause people to copy the work of others without getting permission and giving credit, called *plagiarism*.) They may be lazy or disgusted with all the work they have to do. Or they like to take risks. They may rationalize that it isn't doing anyone any harm. Or they see examples of cheating by people they respect, perhaps their parents, on taxes or work hours or reporting expenses.

The effects of cheating can be damaging to you and to the possibilities of living well with people. Each time you cheat and get away with it, you are more of a "cheater" than you were before. You're more likely to cheat again. You probably feel bad about yourself. That makes you hard to live with. (If you don't feel bad about yourself, you have a real problem. You're getting into deeply damaging habits.) Also, when it becomes known that you cheat—and it will—you get a bad **reputation**.

Despite all this, many people do cheat. If you're one of

them, here are some suggestions. Talk over the problem with someone who may help you make up your mind to stop and help you stick to your decision. Admit your cheating, explain as best you can why you cheated, and take the consequences. Doing this will, in the long run, win people's respect. If, despite your best efforts, you lapse and cheat again, don't feel that you are forever lost. Admit it, deal with it, and start again. You can change. If you find it hard not to cheat on tests because people are seated so close together, bring the subject up in class for discussion, or maybe discuss it privately with your teacher. If you are cheating because assignments seem dull and pointless and you feel you have more important things to do, again, talk with your teacher. Perhaps, if you prove you know the material, you can get alternative, more interesting assignments.

If you know someone is cheating, should you tell? See also honesty.

child abuse

You have probably read and heard on TV about "child abuse." Usually the term refers to abuse of younger children, but teenagers also are abused, and so are adults. There is wife abuse, husband abuse, even parent abuse. The most sensational kind of abuse is *sexual abuse*, where children are used by adults for sexual enjoyment, usually involving the touching and fondling of sexual parts of the body and sometimes sexual intercourse. Other kinds of abuse are *physical abuse*—striking and hurting the bodies of the young—and *psychological abuse*—yelling at, insulting, or putting down young people so that they feel terrible about themselves (even laughter can be a method of psychological abuse). Most child abuse happens at home, but sometimes it happens also at school.

If you find yourself the object of abuse, especially sexual abuse, don't go along with it. It's not the sort of situation you should try to live with. Get help; tell somebody, no matter what threats have been made to keep you quiet. Also, tell the person who is abusing you that you object to what is happening, and then stay away from that person. Tell your parent. Tell a relative or trusted neighbor. Or tell a school counselor or nurse or teacher. For help, you can dial a free national hotline, 1-800-4-A-CHILD, or you can look in the white pages of your telephone book under Child Abuse for a local number. See also **incest**.

chores

In every house and around the yard there are routine jobs that need to be done on a fairly regular basis. If these chores aren't done, things get to be a mess and life becomes difficult. The same goes for many classrooms and schools, except that quite often special people are paid to do chores in school.

Typical chores at home are buying food, preparing food, setting the table, serving food, clearing the table, washing up after meals, collecting trash, emptying garbage, housecleaning (both people's own rooms and rooms and areas used by everybody), caring for pets, doing minor repairs, mowing grass, raking leaves, and weeding. As a general rule, there are more chores than people want to do, and often it becomes a matter of **negotiating** an arrangement so that everyone does his or her share—a division of labor. It's quite natural that from time to time family members will feel they are being made to do more than their fair share of disagreeable jobs. (See **unfairness**.)

In some families, it works very well for the mother to do most of the inside cooking and cleaning and the father to do the repairing and outside yard work, with both parents farming out jobs to the children as they think best and according to the kids' interests and abilities. (See **sex roles**.) In other families, however, it works better to have a plan more or less agreed to by everyone. You may all sit down together, draw up a list of jobs, and then decide who should do what and on what schedule. It's a good idea to work out a plan for shifting chores around so that nobody gets stuck too long with the same dull job. (Some families write each chore down on a separate card and then redistribute the cards from time to time, allowing family members to take turns choosing from the pile.) Also, letting people trade chores if they want to is useful. It can provide for changes of schedule in life outside the home.

Sometimes, a chore doesn't get done for a good reason—or a bad one—and people give excuses for not doing it. Excuses should be listened to and respected if they're legitimate. Also, often it is fun to do chores together: for instance, washing and putting away the dishes. This provides a very good time for **talking things over**, either solving family problems or just exchanging ideas and feelings.

Usually there has to be someone who decides whether or not a person has done a good enough job on a chore: dishes can be "washed" and still be dirty; living rooms can be "cleaned" and still look a mess. In most families, the adult who spends most time in the house sets these standards, and it's important, if you're to live well together, that people not be allowed to get away with a sloppy job.

One special aspect of chores is **your room**. Do you have a right to leave your own place a mess if you close the door and it doesn't affect the lives of family members? This can be a complicated question.

Here are two ways to improve family relationships concerned with chores: Don't dawdle; do your chores on schedule or explain why you didn't. And now and then offer to help someone who obviously needs it. ("Hey, Mom, I'll do the cleanup tonight. I haven't got much homework.") If you feel you are being pressed to do more than your fair share, find a time to say so, calmly and factually. If you are being exploited, your parents are probably not aware of it and need to know.

Some people enjoy doing the definite, useful, routine tasks that chores are. But more often chores are a minor burden to be borne. It may help if you remember that they provide a way to learn about **responsibility**, and they are good practice for later in life, when **jobs** may require good habits and doing work well, thoroughly, and on time. (*See* **goals**.)

Chores at school are usually a much smaller part of life

than chores at home, but they can provide opportunities for living well with teachers. If you are assigned a chore (erasing the chalkboard, picking up litter, sweeping a corridor, distributing teaching materials, or whatever), do it well and with a smile. If you see something that needs to be done, sometimes volunteer to do it. (If you're worried about how this may look, read **teacher's pet**.) If there are lots of chores to be done and no one seems to be doing them very well, find a private time to talk with your teacher about it, maybe along with two or three classmates, and offer to help work out a plan to improve matters. Some of the suggestions about chores at home may be useful at school too.

Last, it may help you to know that it's quite normal to resent having to do chores. So go ahead and feel resentful! Then think about it and see the necessity of the chores—and *do them*.

clothes see appearance

communication

Obviously, if you want to live well with people, you've got to communicate with them, to share ideas, **feelings**, problems, and satisfactions as well as basic information about daily life. You have one life, but it's divided into parts—home, school, friends. Your parents' lives are also divided—home, job, friends, the community. It's very easy for people to get so involved in some part of their lives the others don't know about that gradually they drift apart. Therefore, help your parents, by opening up all you can and by asking them to.

There are a number of blocks to communication. Here are a few: giving **orders**, threatening, preaching, lecturing, judging people, **blaming**, name-calling, ridiculing, sulking, walking out, **yelling**, laughing *at* people, lying, changing the subject. Obviously, some of these things can also be useful ways to communicate, but most of the time they tend to shut it off. *See also* **arguments; talking things over; time together**.

"Dear Abby"

A way of communicating feelings or problems indirectly is to play the "Dear Abby" game. All the players write a "personal problem" letter—it can be a real problem or a made-up one—to Abby, signed with a fictitious name (like "Ruined in Chicago" or "Mother's Slave"). Exchange letters, and have each person write down an answer as helpfully and briefly as possible. (Start "Dear Ruined" or "Dear Momslave.") Then have the letters and replies read aloud. This game is a lot of fun and provides for some good communication that doesn't threaten anyone.

competition

Competition is a complicated subject. To *compete* means to work hard to accomplish something, to achieve one or more **goals**; but it also means to strive against someone else as a rival in an effort to win, as athletic teams do, or as you do in a game.

At home, it is often fun to compete against your parents in games. That's healthy, and during games is often a good time to get in some **communication** too. But it is certainly not healthy to compete against your parents for their **love**. You need their affection and support, and they need yours. If there seems not to be enough to go round, this is something you need to talk about. It doesn't help at all to feel as if your parents ought to love you more, and therefore love each other less! Love begets more love; it's not a limited quantity.

However, time—the hours in a day—may be something that you do feel the need to compete for. In a busy family, children often believe they aren't getting their share of time to talk and be listened to. If you feel this way, say so and try to work out a plan. Often you can find time when you share **chores** together (like washing the dishes) or while you are driving together in the car. Keep a sort of mental list of things you need to talk about, and use the opportunities when there's no competition. (*See* **time together.**)

Other things family members tend to compete for are **TV** time, **telephone** time, space to put things, **money**—you can think of lots of others. Again, the only sensible way to solve the competition problem is to discuss it, work out a plan, and then stick to it.

Some people think that competition and cooperation are opposites—that you can't be both competitive and cooperative. This idea is mistaken. Obviously, families need to cooperate, to work together. But most people are helped to success and self-respect and satisfaction by competition, too. In the family (and also in school), try to think of competing not against others but with yourself, to reach **goals** or **standards** of excellence. Last time you got 15 out of 25 words right on the spelling test; this time you're going to try for 20. Last time it took you fifteen minutes to gather the trash and put it out for collection; this time you'll try to do it just as well in ten.

One special word about school. If you want to live well with teachers, *never* compete with them for control of the class. They must be in control—not of your mind and feelings, but of the basic order in behavior and discussion. (*See* **arguments; discipline; rules.**) This doesn't mean you must behave like a docile lamb. There's plenty of room for stimulation and discussion, but no place for competition for control.

complaining *see* unfairness

conflicts

In any situation where people live together there are bound to be conflicts, ranging from who gets to use the bathroom or telephone to really major differences about behavior and possessions and **goals**. Conflicts are a normal part of the rub of life. You can be sure of one thing: rarely, either at home or at school, will you get your conflicts solved once and for all. The best you can do is work on them.

In a moment, we'll talk about a way to settle conflicts, but first here's an alphabetical list of ways that don't work.

As you read each word, ask yourself, "Do I act this way in conflicts?" (If you answer *no* to every one, you're probably not being honest!) The list: apple-polishing, blaming, bossing, buckling under, bullying, cheating, conforming bitterly, defying, dominating, dropping out, fantasizing, fighting, groaning, hitting, nagging, pretending (that everything's all right), pushing, rebelling, resisting grimly, scolding, snarling, trying to win, yelling. (*See also* **arguments; fights; rebellion.**)

OK, that's the nasty list. Now here's a good method of getting conflicts eased and sometimes solved. It works at home and at school. It works with a whole family or a whole class or just between two people. You might suggest it to your parents and teachers (or siblings and classmates). It can't be done in a great hurry. You have to find a time when you can get together, take the telephone off the hook and talk. (*See also* **negotiating.**)

Conflict Resolution

Step 1: Define the problem. Example: Arguments about clothes. You and your parents can't agree on clothes for parties, clothes for school, clothes for around the house. Be as specific as possible. At this stage you're describing the problem, not solving it, so there's nothing to argue about.

Step 2: Brainstorm solutions. Examples: Everybody has to pass inspection in the morning. . . . Try total freedom, wear what you want. . . . Write lists of what people find annoying or unsuitable. . . . Have a complaint hour just before supper. . . . Buy a big mirror and put it by the front door or in the kitchen so people can see what they look like . . . Call in a clothing consultant. . . . Wear what you want *if* it doesn't annoy anyone else and is OK for the situation you're going into. . . . Be more frank with each other. . . . Don't allow *any* criticism . . . and so on. As you can see, any idea is acceptable for consideration, no matter how crazy.

Step 3: Evaluate the solutions. Go over the various items on the brainstorm list. Cross off those that won't work, or change them until they might work. Add to the list if new ideas occur to you. Try to end up with an idea or set of ideas that might work. *Note:* Nobody's scolding or fighting; everybody's thinking—using their brains—and trying to solve the problem.

Step 4: Agree on a solution. This may be difficult, but not as difficult as when you just argue about it. And the fact that you all have had a chance to express your ideas makes everyone readier to agree. An example of a solution for the clothing conflict might be: Wear what you want if it doesn't annoy anyone and is OK for the situation; be frank with each other; get a big mirror. It often helps to write down the solution and post it somewhere, under a heading: CLOTHING AGREEMENT, NOVEMBER 5, 1986.

Step 5: Commit yourself to trying the solution. Promise to do your best to behave according to the solution for a certain amount of time: say, two weeks.

Step 6: Meet again and discuss how the solution is working. If it's working, great. If not, go through the process again and improve the solution. After all, circumstances change.

criticism

Nobody's perfect. As you look at yourself and those around you, you can see that, and when you see it you're likely to criticize. Criticism can be very useful; it helps us improve. But criticism can also be discouraging and make us feel angry or resentful or both, and when we're that way we're not easy to live with.

One of the most powerful kinds of criticism is *self-*criticism. Teenagers are especially likely to think things like "I'm no good at anything"; "Why can't I ever look right?";

criticism

"I'm so dumb"; "Nobody likes me." People who feel that way about themselves aren't much fun. On the other hand, to sort of stand off and look at your own behavior and appearance critically and objectively is very useful. You can see things about yourself that are great and feel happy about them, and you can see things about yourself that could be improved and work on them.

There is also criticism of others, probably more frequent—and certainly more noticeable—than self-criticism. It, too, can be very harmful and very useful. Here are some suggestions for making it helpful. Criticize behavior—what people do, how they act—rather than the people themselves. For example: "Dad, for the last two nights the noise of your TV really came between me and my homework" or "That complaint about my lying on the living-room floor annoyed me, Mom," rather than "Dad, you must be deaf or something the way you turn up the TV" or "You just can't stand seeing a person lying down, Mom."

Make your criticisms specific rather than general. Never say, "You always . . . " or "you never . . . " *Always* and *never* are hard to take and probably not accurate.

Choose your moment to criticize, usually when people are relaxed and you aren't angry. However, pointing out a specific example can be useful, as, "Dad, excuse me, but right now that TV is messing up my science problems"—and smile!

Make your criticisms in the form of suggestions rather than complaints or demands. And don't criticize too frequently, or it becomes nagging.

Accept criticism in a positive way, if you can. "Mom, am I ever glad you told me my feet smelled and made me change my socks. We were really crowded in the music room today, and the person next to me had really smelly feet. It was repulsive." Now and then, ask for criticism about how you act or look or talk—or anything else. It makes it easier for others to give you good suggestions, and it also makes them feel better if you have a criticism for them. *See* **praise.**

curfew *see* hours

cursing

Cursing, or swearing, means using "bad" language. It doesn't usually help people live well together. It may be harmless among good friends, but it probably doesn't go in most families, and you should never curse in class. The effect of the words you use depends on the situation and the feelings of the people you use them with.

Here are some suggestions about cursing. If you can avoid it, do. If you can't, because it helps you feel better, curse in private, but be careful that it doesn't become a habit that carries over into public. It's less harmful to say "Damn!" than "Damn you!"; or "Hell!" than "Go to hell!" The former are just words, the latter are directed at people.

You may be able to get satisfaction by using milder words with great feeling, words like "Gee!" or "Golly!" or "Gosh!"—but they do seem pretty tame. A friend of mine who feels he should never say "Shit!" has invented a special couple of words that give him satisfaction and only amuse others. He exclaims, "Peach pits!" And I've heard a farmer say, "I don't give a *sheep dip* for that!" Read more under **language**.

dating

Dating and going steady are common among teenagers, and that's as it should be—and will be, no matter what adults do or don't do. But *not* dating and *not* going steady are also common, and that too is as it should be. Many teenagers just aren't interested, or, tough as it may be to admit, they can't get dates with people they like. And yet teenagers who have never dated or gone steady do go on to college, job, and life, and most of them get married. Further, very few high school dates result eventually in marriage, no matter how intense and permanent the feelings of love may seem at the time. All these are facts that you and your parents (and your dates, if any) can usefully talk about.

Dating and going steady give people practice in getting

to know others in a close, intimate way. There's a sense of security in going steady. You have somebody to go to parties, dances, and movies with, and somebody you can comfortably share ideas and feelings with. Going steady, however, if it's too steady, can prevent you from knowing different kinds of people. It can be boring to act almost like "an old married couple" when you're in your teens. Discuss these things, too, with your parents. You can talk about them in general if you don't want to share all the details of your private life. At least, general discussion will show your parents you're thinking about these matters, and that will ease their fears—and who knows? You might even learn something from your parents' experience and opinions.

Two other facts about dating and going steady: they are a very common cause of **arguments** and **conflicts** between teenagers and parents, and many parents are really frightened about what they might lead to. What follows may help you and your parents deal well with those possible conflicts and fears.

First, explain why you want to date or go steady, if you do. Then, introduce your date to your parents, if possible the first time you have a real date, or even before that, and be sure your date does the same for you with his or her parents. Allow time for some conversation between your parents and your date. Don't just rush into the living room, say, "This is Susie, Mom and Dad, and we're late for the movie!" and rush out. Expect your parents to ask questions of your date (sort of vital statistics—age, parents, interests). Don't take it as the third degree, it's based on care and love and concern for you.

Be sure you tell your parents in advance where you're going, how you're getting there and back, and what time you expect to be home. (*See* **rules; transportation**.) Talk this over with your date so there will be good understanding. If you or your date is driving the car, assure your parents that you both know about the dangers of mixing driving and drinking. (*Fact:* The highest accident rate is among under-21 drivers.)

Early in your dating relationship, spend some time at home—yours and your date's—so that both sets of parents feel comfortable. (This doesn't mean that parents have the right of approval or disapproval, date by date, but you are their child and they properly feel a strong sense of responsibility for you.) Also, early on, discuss with your parents questions of **sex** and assure them you know enough so that nobody's going to get pregnant or impregnate anyone. (If you don't know enough, stay away from intimate sexual behavior, which you may well believe in staying away from anyway.) By taking the initiative in talking about all this, you can maintain the right of you and your date to privacy.

death

It's normal to be afraid of death, both your own death and the death of your parents and grandparents. It can seem strange and terrifying to think that someday people we love may not be here any longer.

When a family member is dying or dies, the time is very stressful, both to you and the rest of the family. You can help, if it feels right, by sharing your grief, your feelings of sadness and loss. You can also be especially useful around the house. If it seems welcome, help with such things as cleaning and cooking and keeping things going smoothly. When people lose their husbands or wives it is quite common for them to cry, to feel depressed, to sleep poorly, to be forgetful, to lose their appetite, and even seem to lose interest in life in general. They may behave in these ways for as long as a year, but they get over it. During this period of grieving, they'll need your support and help.

And you yourself will probably suffer some of the same symptoms of grief. Share your feelings. Work through it together with your parent. Ask your parent to help you, too. It may be a very welcome request, an opening for sharing.

Even worse than death, quite often, is the process of dying. When a closely loved person lingers on and suffers, it's very hard not only on the dying person but also on those who observe the process. Again, you can try to be especially helpful at home. Make it possible for your parent to visit the dying person. Also, take the initiative yourself to visit. We know how much such visits, especially from young people, mean to the dying, even if they aren't able to say so, except maybe by a small smile, a special look, or a squeeze of your hand.

When you do visit someone who is very ill or dying, if you're with someone else, be sure to talk to the dying person, not just to your fellow visitor in the presence of the person. Don't be falsely cheerful. Give news about what's going on, even if there's no response. Ask how the person feels, and listen and watch hard for a reply. If you can do it naturally, say how much you love and appreciate the person. Hold the person's hand if that seems welcome, or touch the person as you are together. Most older people in distress love to be touched. When you speak, face the person and speak clearly, but don't shout. Remember, it's OK just to be together, touching in silence. Dying people, inside, are often much more aware of what's going on around them than they are able to show.

discipline

When Americans criticize schools, which they often do, the most common complaint is "lack of discipline." To the critics this seems most often to mean that students don't sit still, keep quiet, obey **rules,** do their homework, and learn the basics: to read, to write, and to do arithmetic.

When Americans talk about families, again they often complain about lack of discipline: children don't do what they're told, speak only when spoken to, and grow up to be models of perfection.

If you want to live well with teachers and parents, you've got to try to understand why so many adults feel this way. Much of the adult world is truly fearful of a disobedient, undisciplined bunch of teenagers, and the simplistic response to the fear is: clamp down!

It's interesting to see how good dictionaries define the word *discipline*. As a noun it means: (1) punishment; (2) training to make people good and competent; (3) external control; (4) a set of rules of conduct. As a verb it means: (1) to punish or penalize; (2) to train; (3) to control. Fortunately, later in the dictionaries, there is an entry, *self-discipline:* correction or control of oneself in order to improve oneself—and in order to protect others from the damage done by people out of control. It's a good idea to find an opportunity to discuss these definitions with your parents and teachers.

There's no doubt that the best discipline is *self-*discipline. If children and teenagers are brought up totally under the control of others—teachers, parents—they are unlikely to learn to control themselves. When we grow up and leave the family and school, "our only chaperon is our own character"—or the community or the law, which, if you break it, may end you up in jail. The way to live well with parents and teachers, as far as discipline is concerned, is to discipline yourself.

In school, if you're given free time, use it well. If you're supposed to be quiet in class, *be* quiet, but if you have something to say, raise your hand, be recognized, and then say it. Ask for opportunities to show self-discipline: **free time** for projects; free time between classes *if* you use it well; a share in considering the rules of the school.

At home, accept the fact that it's your parents' (or parent's) home; you share it, but the main **responsibility** for what happens there is the parents'. Don't challenge this. Instead, ask for chances to show self-discipline: useful things you can do, free time you can use well. If you can't discipline yourself, expect to be disciplined by your parents. Accept the **punishment** you may receive, but ask for a chance to talk about it and maybe work out your own punishment. And if discipline from parents seems unreasonable or even hateful, accept it (hard as that may be!) and then find a time to talk about it.

divorce

Obviously, divorce and how to live with, or away from, divorced parents and stepparents is too difficult and complicated to be treated fully in a few paragraphs. But there are some important and helpful ideas to set forth. The first is that divorced parents or stepparents are essentially no different from a person's own married parents. They are human beings, easy and difficult to live with, all different from each other. The joys and problems of living with them are the same as those of living with other parents—except that they've been through a divorce. For some people, divorce is a shattering experience; for others it isn't—one can't generalize.

In the United States, divorce is a common experience. In the past ten years, the marriage rate has been about 10.5 per thousand people; the divorce rate has been about 5 per thousand people. About 4 out of every 10 marriages will end in divorce. But getting divorced probably doesn't mean that your mother and father don't like marriage. They—or at least one of them—didn't like the particular marriage they were in. Most divorced people get married again. In fact, marriage is a very popular institution. About 93 percent of Americans get married. Being married to a right person (note I didn't say *the* right person) is, most of the time, far better than not being married. But being married to a wrong person can be hell. Try to keep these facts in mind as you figure out how to live with divorced parents and remarried parents.

Another point: Many children, teenage and younger, are afraid that every time their parents argue or yell or squabble it means they are about to get divorced. Remember that **arguments, criticism,** and **yelling** are often just a normal way for a couple to express their **feelings**—a way of **communication,** probably a lot better than bitter silence. If you are afraid that your parents' arguments may mean a divorce in the offing, find a time to ask one or both of them about it and be prepared to listen.

Yet another point: Remember that whether or not your parents get divorced is beyond your control. You can't keep them together if they want to separate, and it's *not your fault* if they do. Furthermore, you won't be able to bring them back together, no matter how much you may want to or how hard you try. You have to learn to get along

divorce

with them, together or apart, and they with you. Of course, you may be a factor in the situation. There are men and women who enjoy being married together until they have children. But then it turns out that they just aren't mature enough, or unselfish enough, to deal with the complications of spouse *and* children. But, again, this isn't your fault. You didn't ask to be born. Furthermore, sometimes a parent—usually it's the father—just decides, for a selfish childish reason, to leave (run away from) the responsibilities of child raising. There's no need for you to feel guilty because of that parent's immaturity, and you're under no obligation to love him (or her) for it. In fact, it would be quite natural for you to feel hatred. You just have to learn to accept the feeling.

Often it's tough to be the child of divorced parents. It's hard to live with the hostility and bitterness before and after the divorce. It may feel awful to have to try to explain it all to your friends (but you *don't* have to; remember that). It feels awful, if you love both your parents, to have to choose which one you're going to live with—which one gets "custody" of you. You may hate the feeling that your parents are competing for your love, maybe even trying to buy it. Also, it's usually hard to have to adjust to two families instead of one—all that shifting and visiting and lugging your things around. Well, admit it's hard and stand up for your needs. *Explain* what you need. *Refuse* to be a tool. Also, it's often very hard to have to take on new siblings, who may be very different from you and have to adjust to you, too. Furthermore, there may be sexual problems that arise, between new siblings or between stepparents and stepchildren. If this happens, assert your rights to your own body, reject sexual approaches, and get help from outside if your own parent can't provide it. (*See* **child abuse**.)

If there's a divorce in the offing, remember that it doesn't mean the end of the world for you. *You are still you;* you have your strengths and your weaknesses. Experience shows that kids do survive their parents' divorce, usually quite successfully. (Look around you at those you know who have survived and are doing well.) Life after divorce is certainly better than having to live in an atmosphere of tension and hostility with two people who have come to hate each other. And some children of divorce find they positively enjoy the extended "family" they are a part of—four parents, more brothers and sisters and grandparents, more choices, more ways to have fun and make life interesting.

Here are some suggestions to help you deal with divorce and the people and problems involved. When you're in doubt, ask for facts and express your feelings and thoughts about them. Also, be sure to listen to the thoughts and feelings of others. Say how you feel. If you can't say it within the family, find someone else you can talk to. Ask for professional help if you feel you need it. Read an excellent book, *Stepkids,* by Ann Getzoff and Carolyn McClenahan.

At school, or in the community, find or start a children-of-divorced-parents support group. This is a small group in which you can share experiences and feelings, and it makes many teenagers feel much stronger and more confident as they face their problems.

Remember, you're not required to love everybody involved in a divorce or remarriage. You can choose. However, it's better to try hard to avoid out-and-out hostility. Don't allow yourself to be *used* as a messenger between your divorced parents. The communication is their responsibility, not yours. (Unfortunately, there are some parents who use their children as sympathetic listeners, almost like psychiatrists, to unload their feelings on. If this gets to be too much of a burden for you, say so!) If you find that living with either of your parents just doesn't work, no matter how hard you try, explain this and see if you and they can agree on a family that you would feel comfortable living with—a sort of foster family.

It will probably be a good idea to tell your teacher or guidance counselor or school principal that your parents are getting divorced. It's a difficult time for you and may affect your schoolwork. (On the other hand, if you feel you can handle school matters perfectly well, you're certainly under no obligation to tell people at school.)

No matter what happens, no matter what living arrangements are worked out, no matter what the strains and stresses are, remember that *you are you,* with your strengths and weaknesses and needs.

drinking *see* alcohol

drugs

If you want to live well with parents, with teachers, with your friends, or with yourself, don't start taking drugs, no matter what pressures may be put on you or how much you think you'd just like to try and see what all those good feelings are. *Don't start!* (Of course, I'm talking about nonmedicinal drugs, not about the medicines used to cure or prevent disease.)

It is a fact—but not a simple fact—that one drug, say marijuana, or pot, which may be harmless, is likely to lead a person to using harder drugs, and these are likely to lead to addiction. Addiction means you're stuck—you can't get off the drug, either because it has become so much a part of your life that you just don't want to give it up (*psychological addiction*) or because your body *must* have it or there are serious physical reactions and great suffering (*physical addiction*). Addiction often leads to crime in order to get money to support the habit; it also can lead to insanity, inability to study or to hold a job, even suicide. Don't start! The promised "good feelings" aren't worth it.

If you feel tempted to use drugs, or are pressured by friends, or are called "chicken" because you won't, do talk with your parents, even though you know what they'll say. If you have a teacher in whom you can confide, talk to that teacher. Ask for information and get yourself fully informed before you start on any drug. A good book to read is *Chocolate to Morphine: Understanding Mind-Active Drugs,* by Andrew Weil and Winifred Rosen.

The item about **alcohol** said that it is the most-abused drug in the United States. Partly this is because its use is such a widely accepted part of our culture. If you are going to be a *teetotaler* (one who does not drink any alcohol at all, ever), good. If not, talk with your parents and, if need be, with a health teacher or a doctor about how to use alcohol responsibly, once you are old enough to do so legally, and how to recognize if you are an alcoholic, for which the only remedy (not cure) is never to take another drink.

dying see death

embarrassment

We all know what it is to be embarrassed (even if we can't spell the word). We do something foolish, or we think it's foolish, or somebody we live with does something that makes us feel foolish and confused and ready to crawl under the table. If you live in a typical family, undoubtedly you have many times been embarrassed by your parents—when they shout; when they ask too many questions; when they tell something secret about you; when they're too friendly or too cool to a friend of yours; when they look sloppy or too dressed up, for example—and your parents have been embarrassed by you—when you shout, ask too many questions, and so on.

The best way to deal with embarrassment may sometimes be to say, right then, "Aw, Mom! *Please*!" But if you can stand it, wait till later and then report the embarrassment. Chances are your parents didn't realize you were being embarrassed. Tell them, maybe with a bit of good-humored laughter, and usually they'll try not to do it again. Then, to be fair and make things better, ask, "Well, OK, since we're on the subject, are there some things that I do that embarrass *you*?" Both you and your parents could write down lists of the things done or said that embarrassed each of you—maybe in the last month—and share them.

There's one special source of embarrassment common among teenagers, and that's their own bodies. Parents are used to your body. After all, they've diapered it, toilet-

feelings 48

trained it, dressed and undressed it, and been used to seeing it around for quite a few years. But they need to know that when you reach **adolescence** and your body begins to mature sexually, you rather quickly start to wish for privacy. Get up your courage and say so. And respect your parents' privacy, too.

To get along well at school, it helps if you and your teachers are aware of what embarrasses the other. If a teacher gives you too much **praise** before the whole class, you may feel like **teacher's pet**. Find a time to tell the teacher this. On the other hand, many teachers are embarrassed by a challenge to the orderliness of their classroom or by being shown to have made an error. Teachers, many of them feel, just aren't supposed to make mistakes. A frank discussion now and then about what embarrasses you and your teachers can be very useful.

escape *see* running away

examinations *see* tests

excuses *see* blaming

feelings

A very important part of our lives is how we feel. If we're coming down with a cold, we usually feel miserable and grouchy. We're probably hard to get along with. If a couple of bad things have happened to us—failing a test, a mean **put-down** from someone, being ignored by a friend, losing something—again, we feel bad. These sorts of feelings affect how we get along with others, including parents and teachers. It's useful to know how others feel, and it's useful to let others know how we feel.

Quite a few people have a sense of **guilt** about how they feel. They think their feelings are somehow "their fault." Actually, almost never is a feeling your fault. *You are not responsible for your feelings.* You are responsible for your *acts*, what you do. "I really feel like screaming!" you may say to yourself, or "I could strangle Jim for acting that way!" or "I feel like getting out of this house [or this classroom, or this school] and never coming back!" It's natural to feel like that sometimes, and you can't just decide not to feel that way. The feeling comes whether you want it or not. *But* if you act the way you feel: actually scream; actually strangle Jim; actually run away for good—those *acts* are your **responsibility**. It's comforting to know that we are not responsible for our feelings and we need not feel guilty about them, even though we may want to work on them a bit, since strong feelings often do lead to actions.

Here are some specific suggestions: Watch people's **body language.** Often how they stand or sit or walk or breathe gives you clues to how they are feeling. Now and then, ask people how they feel: "How did you feel when . . . ?"; "How do you feel today, I mean really?"; "When I do [whatever it is], do you mind or do you feel OK about it?" Then, when people tell you how they feel, be sure you're **listening.** There are different ways of saying "Fine" or "OK" or "Pretty well." It often helps to try to repeat back to people what you think they expressed. "You really feel angry, I guess"; "You're sad Dad's away, aren't you?" The technical term for this is to *reflect* a person's feelings. Often it makes them feel good and feel understood.

Never—well, hardly ever—deny a person's feelings: "You aren't really angry"; "The way I keep my room [or chew gum, or talk in class, or stuff my mouth with food] doesn't really bother you." If someone denies your feelings, say as calmly as you can, "No, I do *feel* that way. I feel . . . " And if you're feeling pretty generally grouchy or tired or sick, warn people, with a smile: "I'm feeling pretty punk today, so I advise you to be careful" or "I've got a test coming up, so I may not be my usual sweet self."

Don't always say how you feel. Sometimes it doesn't make you easy to live with if your mother and teacher know that you feel like strangling them. Also, a constant reciting of feelings can get to be pretty boring. But when your feelings are hurt, say so sometimes. It's amazing how often *feelings* 50

people are unaware of how other people feel. And if you ever get the feeling that everybody's doing everything wrong but you, watch it! The trouble is probably inside you.

Sentence Completion

As a way of sharing feelings, play the sentence-completion game. With your family, or in class, write the beginning of a sentence on a large piece of paper or on a chalkboard and then ask each person to complete it. (You can use more than one sentence if you have more to say.) Some sample beginnings are: I'm proud of . . . ; I wish I could . . . ; Right now I'm afraid of . . . ; What really embarrasses me is . . . ; What bugs me these days is . . . ; If I could change one thing [or three things] around here, I'd . . . Ask people to suggest sentences to complete.

Sometimes it helps to write down your feelings instead of blurting them out. Some well-known person said, "How can I know what I think till I see what I write?" Writing clarifies things and puts them into perspective. Also, sometimes the act of writing them down makes you feel better, or understand better. Once you've written down how you feel, put the paper aside for a day or two. If the feelings still need to be shared with parents or teachers, perhaps showing what you've written may help. However, don't forget that when something is in writing, it exists to be examined and reacted to. Thus it could be very helpful to share, *or it could be so definite that it causes trouble.*

Making Faces

This may seem silly but quite a few people have found it useful and fun. If you're feeling bad about something, sit down alone in front of a mirror and make all the faces you can that show how you feel. Make them in as exaggerated a way as you want to. You can also use hand and arm gestures to add to the body language, but no words!

You can also sit opposite another person, or a small

group around a table, and make a face, as funny or grim as you want, and then ask each person first to tell how you're feeling and then to say what they think might make you feel that way. Go around the group with faces and reactions.

fights

As with **arguments** and **yelling,** fighting can be a way of genuine **communication** within a family. If two people fight about something, it's clear that the matter means a lot to them. That's a message. Or if a person suddenly—or gradually—starts to fight during an argument or conversation, it probably means you're getting close to something painful about his or her life and you'd better be careful. That too is a message. You can get the same sorts of messages at school from teachers—except that teachers rarely fight, except with words or **punishment,** actual or threatened. Be alert to these messages.

Fighting, then, is rather common, and some people may enjoy it some of the time. It can even relieve tensions between people who know each other well. But fighting is bad if it is very frequent; if people's feelings are deeply hurt; if fists, feet, or—even worse—knives are used; if it gets out of control. It's no crime to *feel* like fighting, but if there is danger of bodily harm, just remember the saying, "Your right to hit me on the nose ends where my nose begins."

It's not necessarily a disgrace to lose a fight. In fact, quite often it helps a relationship if you just give up and say, "OK, you win." If you do give up and yet feel that what you were fighting for was really all right, then, as you admit defeat in the fight, say, "We need to talk about this." And keep alert for a good calm time when you can talk. See *also* **competition; conflicts.**

free time

Everyone—teenagers, parents, teachers—needs time to do nothing, to have fun, to goof off. It's good to remember this about your parents when, even if there's a lot of work to do, they just relax and do nothing. The same goes for teachers. If they're in their classroom and the door is closed, understand it if they don't seem to want to talk with you. Just ask, "When can we talk?" Also, they may not be doing nothing; they might be marking papers or thinking and planning.

You, too, need some free time, no matter how far behind you may be in your duties or how heavy your **work load**. If your parents question this, explain your need and they'll understand. A good plan is to offer yourself a reward after, say, ninety minutes of work: fifteen minutes of snacking and comics or one TV program. If necessary, explain the plan so that your parents will understand.

However, if you have a great deal of free time, you can expect to be questioned about it. One of the fears of parents and teachers is either that you're wasting too much time or that in free time, unsupervised, you may get into trouble. That's why many families and all schools have **rules** about where you should be and what you may do during extended periods of free time. It can help you all get along better if you explain what you're doing in your free time, but also explain your need for it. You need to relax; and you learn **responsibility** for yourself during the time when you're free.

friends

There should be no question about it: your friends are yours; *you* choose them, and *you* work on the joys and problems of getting along with them. Your parents can't and shouldn't try to do these things for you, even though there may be ways they can help. But there's also no question that the friends of teenagers are quite often a cause of friction and misunderstanding with parents. Your parents may not like their looks, their language, their habits, or their manners. Or, on the other hand, they may admire some friend of yours so much that they keep asking why you can't be as perfect, polite, interesting, and hard-working as the friend. (*See also* **popularity**.)

Most teenagers find that they relate to their friends quite

differently from the way they relate to their parents and teachers. Parents really aren't just friends, they're much more. They have authority over you; they are responsible for you in a way a friend can't be; and, for better or worse, you're stuck with parents—you have them no matter what. It's fine when you can say, "I really feel my dad's a friend," or "Mom's my best friend when it really counts," but friend is not all they are.

As for teachers, they too may feel very friendly toward you and you toward them, but basically they are professionals. They have a job to do: to teach their students. Only in rare cases do they become mainly friends. If they did, they could never do their jobs.

Here are some suggestions about how friends influence living well with parents. Make a point of having your friends over to your house so your parents can meet them and know who they are. Also, try to meet your friends' parents. If your parents object to some of your friends because they seem so different, find a way to say, "I've got to learn to get along in my world as well as yours," and be ready to talk about that.

Always check in so your parents know your friends are there. Of course, you probably can't do this with every friend you may have, and, as I said, they're *your* friends. If your parents seem to have a real thing about a certain friend's behavior, you might work on your friend a little, not too much, to try to adjust to life at your house. And when any friends come over, tell them about whatever **rules** there may be so that they can respect them—rules about things like **TV,** refrigerator, **telephone, your room, chores.** Also, respect the rules when you go to your friends' houses.

Unless your parents do so naturally (and they may be embarrassed or not want to butt in on your life), suggest that they be positively hospitable: greet, talk, offer food, discuss interesting issues. Be very careful not to let it seem as if your friends are turning you against your parents and their **ideals** and **values.** Exclamations like "But, Mom, *no*body else [whatever it is]!" or "Can't you see that

friends

everybody else . . . ?" should be off the list of things you say. You can explain what your peers do and don't do, but don't suggest that your parents are in the dinosaur age.

Try very hard to avoid long, whispered telephone conversations. Sure, parts of your life are confidential, and of course you need to talk privately with friends, but just remember how it may impress other members of your family. If you have had a long whisper, and it seems to bother your parents, maybe you can set their minds at ease by now and then explaining what you were talking about.

Sometimes when, as do most teenagers, you relate more and more closely to your peers and thus become less and less dependent on your parents, they may feel a little bit abandoned. You can help them by telling them, and showing them, that you love them. Both you and your parents can be comforted to know that many parents whose children have grown up and are out on their own report what a joyous discovery it is when they can relate to their children as very good, intimate, equal friends. It's something to look forward to!

Just a word about friends at school. If you want to get along well with teachers, be careful that your friends don't distract you from your work or from saying "Good morning" to the teacher as you come into class. Also, never pass notes in class or whisper, hoping not to be noticed. It can make teachers feel angry or dull or as if some bad thing were being plotted.

Special note: Don't rely on friends for information about **sex**. It's a good subject to talk and exchange ideas about, but get your facts from a reliable source: a good book, a trained teacher, or a doctor. (One reliable book is my own *Love and Sex in Plain Language*.) Many mistakes that can lead to pregnancy, disease, and bad feelings arise from rumors and wrong information spread among friends, even though the friends are sure that what they say is true.

fun see **free time**

generation gap

Even though we are all human beings—parents, teachers, teenagers—the difference in our ages sometimes can make it harder to live together. Mark Twain recognized this when he wrote, "When I was a boy of 14 my father was so ignorant I could hardly stand to have the old man around. But when I got to be 21, I was astonished at how much he had learned in seven years." And Socrates, 2,400 years ago, complained that young people lacked motivation, were stirred by wild music, and were generally irresponsible. It's inevitable that sometimes the fact that our parents and teachers were brought up in a different generation from ours creates a gap in understanding. It can be a lot of fun, and very useful, to try to cross the gap. Ask your parents and teachers sometimes, "What was it like when you were kids?" This may give you a chance to explain how it seems to you to be different now.

We need to take care not to judge ideas and opinions by the age of those who express them. It can be a real put-down. Don't say, "But, Dad, you're so old-fashioned!" It's a pretty sure way to make him angry and also to fail to understand what he's saying. And if someone, parent or teacher, says, in effect, "You kids, I don't know what the world's coming to," ask for an explanation so that you can understand and maybe even adjust—or explain. Chances are things are really pretty much the same.

goals

Most parents and teachers like to live and work with teenagers who are making an effort to get somewhere in life—who are motivated to achieve worthwhile goals. If you are such a person, three cheers! If, on the other hand, you spend a lot of time in what seems to be aimless goofing off and don't seem to care about achieving anything, your parents and teachers are probably concerned and unhappy. No one can tell you, "Get motivated!" That has to come from inside. But it's never too late to change.

High achievers are most likely to come from families in

which the parents hold high standards for their children and give them the freedom to set their own responsible goals. They provide only the assistance needed for the children to achieve the goals on their own and then give plenty of specific feedback. ("That's a fine job!" rather than "You're a really nice person!")

What are people like who can set good goals and reach them? They are realistic about themselves, not wishful thinkers. They don't assume they can hit a home run every time they come to bat or suddenly get straight A's when before they've only earned C's. They spend time thinking seriously about their goals, both long-term ("What do I want to achieve as my life's work?") and short-term ("How far can I get in this science project by tomorrow after school?") and in-between ("What college should I aim for?"). They set challenging goals for themselves, ones they can probably achieve with hard work and good skill, not easy ones that require little effort.

Then they plan the steps they will take and the equipment they will need. They know how to get and use help when they need it, but they really depend on themselves. They calculate the obstacles they may have to overcome, and if the obstacles are insurmountable, they revise their goals so that they are achievable and then work hard to reach them.

Various techniques help: dividing the task into smaller parts and getting through them one at a time; setting specific work times; checking progress regularly, realistically, and with satisfaction. High achievers are stimulated by a feeling of **competition**—not so much to do better than other people but to do better than they themselves have done before. They are stimulated, too, by a standard of excellence that they hold in their minds and try to meet— the idea of what a good job is—and they occasionally stop and think forward to how good they will feel when they achieve their goal, which helps motivate them to finish. If they achieve their goal, they evaluate their work and try to think of ways they might do better next time. If they fail to reach their goal, they figure out why, learn from the experience—and go ahead to set further goals.

Good, responsible high achievers, especially independent ones, are very pleasing to parents and teachers. One caution, though: Be careful that you don't become so intent on reaching a goal that you are unaware of the effects on others, especially those close to you.

Take a look at your life in terms of what you've just read. Discuss with your parents the ways people achieve. Maybe even suggest to your teachers that the class might consider these matters. Contrary to what many people believe, high achievers tend to be happier, more satisfied, easier to live with, and more useful and fun than low achievers.

going steady see dating

goofing off see free time

grades

Whether on **report cards, tests,** or papers and projects, grades can cause friction and misunderstanding. All of us—students, teachers, parents—could avoid trouble if we considered grades as information, not as some kind of medal or prize. If you get a *B+*, a *C–*, an *F,* an 87, or a 69, what does it tell you? If you aren't sure, ask your teacher to explain. But never complain. Just ask, and if the explanation doesn't satisfy you, say why, but always calmly.

Never beg for a higher grade, even though teachers sometimes make mistakes. However, sensibly discussing your grade sometimes may cause it to be raised, this time or next time. Also, it shows that you care. But before you discuss, be sure you understand the marking or grading system of your school and that your parents do too. You'll find it written down somewhere. If you don't, ask for it—very politely.

Here are some other suggestions. Remember, what is being graded is your performance, not your value as a person. Sometimes, though, how you behave in class affects your grade. (Some schools give a "behavior" grade or an "effort" grade. If your school does, treat those grades, too, as information.) If you aren't sure about this, ask. When graded papers are passed out in class, never say to your neighbors, "Wadja get?" It annoys teachers and it's a much less important question than "What does this grade tell me about my work?" You can always wait till after class to compare.

Show your grades to your parents, even if you aren't required to, and make sure you both understand them. (Be careful, though, about having your parents go to school to complain. By the time you're a teenager, usually it's better to do your own follow-up, not complaining but asking. See **parent-teacher conferences.**) Grades may be seen by your parents as a key to your future, and in part they are. Your academic record will influence where you may go to college or what sorts of jobs you may be able to get. Talk about this with both parents and teachers, if you need to or if your parents are worried.

grandparents

If you're lucky enough to have grandparents within easy visiting distance, they can be a great asset. They can ease some of the difficulties you may have in living with your parents. They are one step removed from any conflicts or problems in your house. Thus, they may be more objective about the problems, not being directly involved. Also, most grandparents really enjoy seeing their grandchildren. One reason they enjoy them is that grandchildren come, and *then they go home!* So visits are rewarding and fun. Grandparents are complimented to be visited and to be asked for advice. Sometimes you may get a bit more advice than you need, but you're not forced to listen to it every day. And the fact that they are even more removed from you in age than your parents are gives them some perspective, and it may give you new points of view. (There's also a double risk of **generation gap.**)

Don't assume, though, that just because they are old

they have unlimited time to give you. Most older people are busy with their own lives. Also, be careful not to use them so much so that you get out of the habit of talking with your parents. That can be harmful. And never ask a grandparent to put in a good word for you. Just be content to visit, share, enjoy, and get some wisdom and, perhaps, a chance to let off steam.

Note: Sometimes aunts and uncles can also serve, and enjoy serving, as needed, objective, loving outsiders.

grief   *see* death

guidance   *see* help

guilt

Guilt is the feeling you have after you've done something wrong, or something you feel is wrong. It's a good thing we human beings feel guilty—feel bad—about doing wrong. If we did not, we'd go right on doing wrong unless we were caught and punished by someone else. In a way, guilt is self-punishment for wrongdoing. It can be an excellent self-regulator, and self-regulation helps us live harmoniously with people.

It may surprise you (and your parents and teachers, if they see this book) to read such enthusiastic words about guilt, for many people think, "The trouble with our society is that people are burdened with so much needless guilt. It's unhealthy!" Well, yes and no. No, because it would be even more unhealthy to feel no guilt after doing wrong. (Some criminals have this disease: they can rob, batter, burn, and kill and feel no guilt. Nothing can stop them but to be caught and imprisoned until they can learn to feel guilty.) But yes, it's unhealthy to feel guilty about things we cannot control. For example, we cannot control our **feelings.** We do not need to feel guilty about them. We cannot control our thoughts. We do not need to feel guilty about them. We may, for a moment, think "I hate you!" about a parent or a teacher. We shouldn't feel guilty about

hating

that feeling, but if we say "I hate you!" directly to the person, that's an action and makes the other person feel bad and perhaps frightened. It's the action we should properly feel guilty about.

Some teenagers (and young children) feel guilty about their parents' **divorce.** That's a needless guilt. Some feel guilty about the fact that they masturbate, or even that they masturbated when they were little children. That's a needless, harmful guilt, unless **religion** is a part of it.

Talking things over is often useful. Sometimes a psychologist or a psychiatrist can give more **help** in talking about the guilt we feel, especially if it's a heavy burden. But on the whole, be thankful for realistic guilt, both your own and that of others.

hating

"Hate" and "hatred" are very strong **words.** They involve intense hostility and loathing, often based on **anger,** fear, or a feeling of having been injured. And yet we sometimes say, "I really hate her," or "I hate Dad when he [whatever he does]" without really meaning it. Students fairly often "hate" a teacher, for a week, or a day, or a minute or two, when they feel the teacher is attacking or injuring them. If you're interested in living well with parents and teachers, be careful how you use the word *hate,* even though you probably don't really mean it in the full sense of its power.

On the other hand, if you feel deep down that you really do hate a parent or a teacher, you probably need **help** in dealing with the emotion. People who are hate-filled can damage themselves. First, talk about your feeling with someone you trust. Perhaps you'll find that the hatred is just for the moment—or the week—and not really serious. If, after talking, you still feel a damaging or dangerous hatred, seek some guidance or counseling from a psychologist or a psychiatrist. Your parents can help you with this, but you'll need to try to explain it to them as well as you can first.

The Hate Game

You can play this delightful game with your family or at school. It's not heavy at all, and it can lead to some good communication, sharing of feelings, and humor. Each player writes down ten hates—things he or she can't stand—like "losing my keys behind the radiator; when the cat jumps on my bed; smells that come from certain places in the house; being laughed at; doing the laundry; seeing that somebody has been in my room; zippers; certain characters down the street; people who sing off-key in the shower; being interrupted when I'm halfway through telling something." Then the papers are folded up and passed to a neutral person, who shuffles them and reads the lists aloud. The rest of the players try to guess who wrote each list. Whoever guesses the most people wins. A variation is "The Love Game." I love: "when I have plenty of clean socks in my bureau drawer; going to horror movies"; and so forth. (This game is fun to play at parties too.)

health

You want to be healthy, your parents want you to be healthy, so what is there to argue about? Where's the problem? It often centers around questions like these: How much sleep should you get? What should you eat? Are you getting enough exercise? What about **smoking**? What about **alcohol** and **drugs**? What about your **appearance**, your complexion? Are you going too far in your **sex** life? Obviously, we can't go into these things here—this is not a health text. But I can urge you to be completely open with your parents about health matters. They probably aren't doctors, and even if they are they shouldn't be *your* doctor, because a doctor needs to be objective about patients. But they do know you well, and if they are kept informed they can help you work out any health problems you may have.

Having an annual physical checkup is a good idea. Your

family doctor, or the doctors at a health center, can give you factual information and advice. It will probably be most useful to go to the doctor with one of your parents, but many teenagers like a bit of time when they can talk with the doctor alone. Be sure you arrange this with your parents in advance. If you suddenly ask to see the doctor alone, your parents may think you have some secrets to hide, so it's better to be as open as possible with them about it. Also, since doctors usually have only a limited amount of time they can give to each patient, it helps to write out a list of questions you want to ask and make an extra copy for the doctor. If your parents have a chance to talk over the list with you before the visit, it helps **communication**. Also try to make a time afterward when you can talk over with your parents what the doctor said.

help

Everybody needs help from time to time, but too much help can be harmful, even objectionable. When you were a baby, you were pretty nearly helpless. All you could do was suck, snuggle, sleep, gurgle, and cry. By the time you're 21, you can expect to be pretty much on your own. As a teenager, you're probably about three quarters along the way from helpless babyhood to self-sufficient adulthood. As you progress toward adulthood, you and your parents should try to keep constantly aware of how much help you need and how much you want to accept.

Adults need help, too, both parents and teachers. If you're to get along with them, you should be aware of what kinds of help they want—and what kinds they don't want.

At home, learn to ask for help if you really need it. Don't just suffer in silence. When you get help, say thanks. Really express your appreciation. Some parents, hoping that teenagers will approach perfection, tend to press more help on their children than they should. So you need to turn down help if you feel you don't need it. Try to do it positively—"I think I can do this myself, but thanks anyway"—rather than negatively—"Leave me alone! What do you think I am, a baby?" This applies especially to homework, which should be called "independent work." Do it yourself, not with your parents or friends.

What about help your parents may need at home? Keep your eyes and ears open, and if you become aware that help is needed, offer it: "Let me [whatever it is] tomorrow. I know you've got a lot of extra stuff to do with Grandma coming." Now and then just ask, "Is there any way I can help?" Even if there isn't, it does wonders for family morale and relationships (see chores).

At school, if you need help with your work or guidance on some problem, do ask for it. Probably the best time is after class or during a homeroom or conference period. However, if you know that quite a few members of the class need help, raise your hand and bring up the problem. This is a part of communication, and most teachers will appreciate it, especially if you already have tried to solve the problem on your own.

As for helping teachers, the best ways are to do your work, raise your hand before speaking, pay attention, be orderly, discipline yourself, and appreciate the good work your teachers are trying to do.

Sometimes people—teenagers, parents, even teachers—find themselves facing personal problems so severe they can't figure out how to deal with them: problems like addiction to alcohol or drugs, the habit of using violence, a constant sense of failure or an actual failure to do the work at school or on the job, a long deep depression and sense of worthlessness, a strong temptation to commit suicide or an attempt to do so, truancy from school, or feeling like running away.

Sometimes deep problems like these can be dealt with by teenagers and parents and teachers working together. But if the problems are really serious and threatening, professional help is needed. One sort of help is provided by *psychologists*. These are people trained to understand how our thoughts and feelings work and affect our behavior. Psychologists give special tests to find out what the problems are, and they consult with those who have problems and give guidance on how to solve the problems or adjust to them. Other specialists, *psychiatrists*, are trained to go even deeper into people's thinking, feelings, and behavior, to help them develop the strength to face their problems and the world they have to live in.

If you think you have very difficult problems, too hard for the usual sorts of discussion and advice to solve, feel free to ask whether you should get some help from a psychologist or a psychiatrist. Or if a parent or teacher or school guidance person suggests professional help for you, be grateful and consider it carefully.

In a sense, these professionals are "rent-a-friends." They have to be paid for, but when you are with them they are absolutely there *for you*. They never punish you. They never threaten you. You can be totally open and frank with them. What you tell them is confidential. You get a special kind of trust from them, a trust you don't have to earn.

hitting *see* arguments; child abuse; fights

homework *see* help; study habits

honesty

A person who is honest is one who tells the truth, who does not deceive or cheat, and who keeps **promises**. There is little question that "honesty is the best policy" for living together. However, sometimes you have to decide *how* to be honest. If you simply tell the whole truth as it comes to you, without thinking about it, you can make life pretty uncomfortable. For example, if you don't like the way your teacher dresses, or your mother's new hairdo, or how your father tells jokes, should you simply say so? No, you shouldn't. You consider the **feelings** of these people; you decide whether or not to tell them what you think, and if you decide to tell, think about when and how. These decisions can be quite complex. "Brutally honest" is a common expression. Be honest, but not brutally so. Tell the truth, but not necessarily the whole truth, unless not telling the whole truth will deceive or be harmful. The best answer to "How do you like my hat?" may be "It's interesting."

Another kind of honesty is to go to a parent or teacher and "tell" on somebody who, say, ate all the cookies, messed up a classroom, cheated on a test, broke a piece of household equipment, or shoplifted some items from a store. This is called *tattling,* or *talebearing.* The tattletale is supposed to do it for pleasure or credit.

Tattling is really giving evidence about something wrong that has been done. Giving evidence is an important part of good living together. Without evidence about who did something wrong, everyone feels uncomfortable, both parents (or teachers) and those others who may be unjustly suspected.

If you are going to give evidence, be certain of your facts. Then, before you tell anyone anything, go to the person who did the bad thing and say that you wish he or she would just admit it and take the consequences. Say that otherwise you're going to have to report what happened. Explain why. Give the person time to think about it. When you do give evidence, if you have to, do it in private and stick to the facts. And if you can, assure the person about whom you gave evidence that you still consider yourself a friend.

hours

How you spend the 24 hours in each day should be a matter of **negotiating** what seems best for all concerned. Your judgment is important, as well as that of your parents. It's only natural that often you will have differences of opinion. The best way to settle the differences is to discuss them, get all the evidence out in the open, and then work on an agreement about schedules, times, limits. (*See also* **rules**.) Try to have the discussion when there's no crisis or hot issue to be debated. And when you agree about your *curfew*—when you have to be home—it's helpful to write down what you agreed so that you all can refer to it.

Of course, agreements aren't engraved in stone. Circumstances change, and when they do, new agreements have to be reached. So keep your parents up-to-date about your needs, and also about the customs of the teenagers you work and play with.

Here are some other points to keep in mind: It's important for most teenagers to have limits set for their hours. It enables them to say, "I've got to go home now. You know, my parents . . . !" A student in eleventh grade once said to a friend in my hearing, "I sure hope my parents are going to refuse to let me use the car this weekend." Therefore, if you don't have limits, *ask* for them, and work them out. The fact that parents set limits—or work them out with you—is a sign that they care for you. For this you can be grateful.

There are vast differences in the amount of sleep individuals need. Some need ten hours a night, some get along on seven or even six. You have to take this into account, both for yourself and your parents. An automatic eight hours is too simple an idea. But if there's a definite disagreement about hours, it's your parents' responsibility to make the final decision. They are the adults and are ultimately responsible. See *also* **parties.**

humor

Seeing the funny side of things can be a real blessing. A sense of humor helps us see life in perspective. A daughter and her mother were arguing bitterly over the daughter's choice of friends and how they behaved, and the mother was grimly making point after point, all of which seemed insulting. Then the daughter realized what a vast hassle they were having—as if the world were coming to an end—about some only medium-sized things, and she smiled at her mother and said, "Gee, Mom, sometimes I think *I'm* the sort of person you don't want me to associate with." They both began laughing and were able to carry on their discussion more in fun.

A sense of humor is an easer of tensions. As pianist-comedian Victor Borge has said, "The shortest distance between two people is a good laugh." If you find yourself saying, or feeling like saying, to your parent or teacher, "That's *not* funny!" stop for a few seconds and see if you can figure out why it seems funny to the other person. On the other hand, if a person has made a bitter, sarcastic remark to you and it really hurts, do say that it doesn't seem funny to you and explain why. Laughing at people can be as bad as hitting them, sometimes even worse. If you suffer in silence it probably won't help.

Remember, too, that some teachers are genuinely concerned about keeping order in their classes and are afraid that too much laughter during a basically serious lesson may get out of control. Try to be sensitive about this, and if you're in doubt about something funny you said, quietly check it out with the teacher after class. "Did you mind when I . . . ?" Most teachers love humor, provided it is relevant to what the class is working on.

Another meaning of *humor* has to do with **moods.** If you or someone at home or at school feels in a "bad humor," it's helpful to say so. We all have a right to be grouchy and difficult sometimes.

Here's a good example of being humorously serious about a situation. A minister was in the middle of his sermon in church one Sunday when the children's class let out and all the youngsters entered the church quietly and sat down with their parents—except for the minister's own son. This boy, feeling at home in the church, ran down the aisle, noisily pretending to be an automobile. Everyone looked in amazement. The minister stopped his sermon briefly and said, "OK, Jimmy, park it and give the keys to your mother." There was a brief happy laugh, a quiet Jimmy, and the sermon continued.

ideals

Ideals are **standards** of perfection, or **goals** we work toward, although few of us, teenagers, parents, or teachers, ever reach an ideal—at least not for very long. But ideals are a very strong force in the lives of most people, a source of power. We strive for them: to be an ideal person, to make an ideal family, to develop an ideal classroom or school. To live well with others we need to try to understand their ideals, what they are striving for, and let them understand ours. We should share our ideals even though we may not always agree on what the ideal way or situation might be.

Some suggestions: Don't expect a person to be ideal. That's painful for others. "Nobody's perfect, not even me." But even though you, your parents, or your teachers can't be ideal, ideals are excellent things to discuss: "What would be the ideal way to learn this subject?" "To have an ideal family, what would we have to do?" "What's the ideal solution to our problem?" Then, when you've got some ideas about ideals, you can work to agree on steps to get nearer to the ideal.

Sometimes there is a **generation gap** in ideals. Parents or grandparents may say, "Now in the good old days . . . " or "When I was young, we . . . " Instead of ignoring such nostalgia for how things used to be, *ask* about it. "How was it?" "What did you do?" It's a good way to learn, and also to understand each other.

Don't force your ideals on others. If you feel strongly about them, try to persuade, not force, and especially try to make your own behavior an example of the ideal. "What you are speaks much louder than what you say," a wise person wrote. And be careful not to act self-righteous as you strive for ideals, as if you were a perfect saint and you are letting everyone know. An old aunt of mine used to say, "A martyr is someone who has to live with a saint." She said it in fun, but she meant it, too. What do you think she meant?

incest

Incest means sexual intercourse or intimate sexual touching between members of the same family, except, of course, between husband and wife. It is a form of **child abuse,** even though the "child" may be sexually mature and well up in his or her teens. There's no question that some members of the same family sometimes feel sexually attracted to others in the family, but it's an attraction that must be denied, rejected, and, if possible, turned off. Incest takes place most often between fathers and daughters, but sometimes between uncles and nieces, brothers and sisters, or mothers and sons. It also occurs in stepfamilies.

If a member of your family attempts to get sexually intimate with you (stroking, deep kissing, touching of your sexual parts), make it clear at once and in words that you won't accept that sort of behavior, and get away from the person immediately. You may be afraid that the person will punish you or withhold some sort of reward from you, or you may fear that it's really your fault—that you shouldn't be so attractive. Nonsense! It's not your fault unless you actively play up to the family member or encourage sexual relations.

If saying *no* and getting away doesn't stop the business, tell someone—your other parent, a trusted relative—and insist on help and support. Don't be scared that this may break up the family. It won't unless the situation is so out of control that it ought to.

Of course, an entirely different kind of affection is the open hugging and kissing among members of a family. That's healthy and very much a part of the way many families show their love toward each other. (Some families don't, and that's OK too.) Also, it's all right, and can be a lot of fun, if fathers and daughters or mothers and sons pretend to flirt with each other—just as a way of saying "You're growing up and are attractive." That's nice to know, a pleasant kind of supportive joking.

A last word: If you should be the victim of incest, it doesn't mean the end of the world for you. It's serious, but most children and adolescents get the help they need or have the strength of character to get over it and go on to live healthy, normal lives, including the parts of life having to do with **sex.**

IQ score *see* tests

jobs

In this book, a job is work you do for pay, not **chores** you're rightly expected to do free as a member of the household. In families that are hard-pressed to find enough money to live on, obviously any added source of income can be a great help. If you can find a paying job and, after keeping a share of your pay for your own needs, turn some money over to your parents for family needs, it's a marvelous contribution and makes life better for everyone. But even if your family doesn't need money from you for basic expenses, holding a paying job can be very good training for life later on, and it will probably make your parents feel good about you and your future. If you do get a job, be sure that it doesn't interfere with your schoolwork or with your chores. Also, if you leave a job after doing well, ask your employer for a written reference for you to keep. You can use references to help get future jobs.

Some teenagers enjoy the sense of independence they gain if they are able to earn enough money to say to their parents, "I really don't need an allowance anymore." If your parents still feel they'd like to continue your allowance, OK; you can put your pay into a bank account and build up reserves for the future. Again, this will probably make your parents feel very pleased.

Some kinds of jobs teenagers hold are gardening, yard work, housecleaning, baby-sitting, selling crafts, hourly work in stores or restaurants, and newspaper delivery. The help-wanted pages in your local paper are a good source of information. Another sort of job you might consider is a household task that your parents would normally pay to have done. I don't mean chores. I mean jobs like painting, or a thorough housecleaning, or a piece of carpentry, electrical work, or plumbing that you think you are qualified to do. You have to prove that you can do it, safely and well. You have to agree on how much you'll be paid. Doing work like this, and the planning that goes into it, can be a great way to get along with your parents, and it also increases your competence and independence.

There is one other thing to discuss about jobs, and that is the lack of one. If an adult is used to working and needs the money for his or her purposes, or for family expenses, and loses a job, it is often a great shock and source of shame, especially for men, whom our culture expects to "support their families." So if one of your parents is unemployed and can't find a job, that parent may become quite hard to live with. People who are discouraged usually are. It's very important, therefore, that you be especially considerate of the feelings of an unemployed parent. Never nag or tease or ridicule. Go out of your way to show respect.

joking see humor

language

You've probably heard parents and teachers say things like "Watch your language!" or "I won't have language like that in here" or "Don't talk that way to me [to her, to him, to anybody]!" There's no question that language can hurt and shock people and drive them apart. Therefore we should "watch" our language—that is, pay attention to the kind of words we use. If we want to live well with others, we must be careful about the language we use with different people and in different situations. There's cursing, "the language of the gutter"; "proper language"; "locker-room language"; "dirty language"; and "classroom language." In most cases, if you're sensitive, you don't speak the same way to your grandparents as to your best friends, even though you love them both. One of the reasons for this is that language changes, and what may be acceptable among teenagers may not be acceptable among older people, even though the older people once were teenagers themselves.

But what a blessing language is! It enables us to explain things to each other, to express our feelings and our ideas, to amuse and entertain each other. That's why I so often suggest that you talk over a problem, discuss it, even sometimes write down solutions—in language that is clear to all. When people who live together decide grimly or bitterly on silence they can't live well together. The same often goes for yelling. (*See* **talking it over; tone of voice.**)

A problem with language sometimes is that we don't understand what a person has said, or we aren't sure. In such cases, don't be afraid to say, "What do you mean? I'm not sure I understand." Or we can ask, "Is this what you mean?" and then restate in our own words what we think the person said. It also can help to say—openly, not bitterly or sarcastically—"Did you understand what I said?" *See* **communication.**

laughter   *see* **humor**

limits   *see* **hours; rules**

listening

Obviously, if you're to live well with parents and teachers, you've got to listen to them. Otherwise, you won't really hear what they say. One of the problems in **communication** is that instead of really listening to each other, we keep thinking, Yes, but . . . or figuring out what we're going to say in reply even before we've really heard what the other person has said. (One teenager complained to her father, "When we talk, every time I take a breath, you put in a paragraph.") People we live with, and we ourselves, feel the need to be listened to and understood. This doesn't mean you have to believe and accept all you hear—you can listen *critically*—but you should try to understand what people are saying. Also, it is useful to respond briefly as people talk with you, to give them feedback: "Yes"; "I see"; "Good idea"; "Uh-huh"; "I didn't realize"; "Wait a sec. Say that again so I can be sure I understand."

It's important, too, to be sure that you are being listened to. If you feel you're not, stop talking and see what happens. Or ask, "Do you understand what I mean?" Don't say "You're *not* listening!" or "You *never* listen to me!" If you really feel you're never being listened to, that in itself *listening*

is a problem that needs talking about, directly and when there's some time. You can't force a person to listen. You can force them to hear—their ears take in the noise—but if they don't want to listen, or their mind is on something else, you won't be listened to.

It also helps to listen to a person's **tone of voice** and pay attention to their **body language**.

Listening in school is a special problem—or opportunity. The very least you can do, if you want to relate well to teachers, is to give the appearance of listening. Look attentive. Look at the teacher, unless you're taking notes. If you aren't understanding, raise your hand quietly and, when you're recognized, ask a question or simply say that you don't understand.

In a classroom you'll spend much more time listening than speaking, and you have to learn to tune in to sounds that come from outside you. You have no control over the speed of your teacher's speaking or of your classmates' discussion, unless, on rare occasions you say, "Wait a minute, please, you're going too fast for me."

Another problem is that your mind can think much faster than anyone can speak, and therefore it tends to wander. A good way to avoid this in class is to jot down important points. But be sure you don't get so busy making a note that you don't hear the next thing.

It's useful to learn certain signals teachers give that something is especially important, like saying "Listen carefully" or "This may be on the test" or "Here are four points" or writing words or key phrases on the chalkboard.

Note: There's one quite common kind of talk in families, and sometimes at school, that you really don't have to listen attentively to, and that's our friendly, easy chatter when we meet one another ("Hi! How are you?" "Wet enough for you?"—that sort of thing) or when we're just chatting and mumbling together without any particular ideas to share. This has been called "conversational clucking," like the noises chickens make when they're secure and safe. It's OK not to listen very hard to such family clucking, but be sure to pay attention if a cluck suddenly turns into a squawk.

Switch Off and Listen

In this game, you switch off your reacting mind as completely as possible and just listen! The other person must then talk about some specific subject that he or she wants to talk about, or that you agree to talk about, for a specific period—say, three minutes. He or she may pause, stop, repeat or whatever, but you remain silent and attentive for the entire three minutes. You, the listener, determine to avoid thinking, "Yes, but..." or "Oh, that's just how I feel," and you don't say, "Uh-huh," "I see," "Yes?" or anything else. You are just attentively silent. It's amazing how much people will say and hear under this special kind of listening situation.

Listen and Recap

This is another good listening game. Here again, you listen hard and attentively, but at the end of each idea expressed by the speaker, he or she stops, and you recap—very briefly—the essence of what you think was said. This is a fine way of discovering whether the speaker is making the ideas clear and whether you are actually hearing what is said. After you've tried this for a while, discuss the results and what you've learned about speaking and listening.

love

One of the seven utterly basic needs of all human beings is love, and one of the kinds of love is *family love*. It's very difficult to live well with parents if you don't feel that they love you and if they don't feel that you love them. Family love doesn't mean that all members of a family constantly feel affectionate toward one another or like the way they behave. In fact, quite often you are probably annoyed, even angered, by the way your parents behave. You may even feel, and perhaps occasionally say, "Gee, I hate it when you [whatever they do]" or "I can't stand the way you [whatever it is]," and when you feel and say these things you mean it! (See **arguments; fights; yelling.**) However, such moments or longer periods of disliking or even **hating** don't mean the end of family love. (And they don't mean the end of love when your parents feel or talk that way toward you, although most parents are mature enough to manage such feelings better than most teenagers can.)

So what is family love? It's a feeling that basically, no matter what, members of a family support and help one another, especially when the going gets tough. It doesn't mean that they always support and approve of everyone's behavior, the way they act. That would be impossible. But as people in the same family, they support and help one another—and most of the time feel a strong mutual fondness. You don't have to deserve or earn family love. You have it because you are part of the family. The poet Robert Frost said it well: "Home is the place where, when you have to go there, they have to take you in."

As a teenager, you may often get so caught up in the trials and problems and turmoil of life that you aren't really aware that you love your parents. So it's good now and then to make yourself aware of it and show your parents you love them. Do something nice for them; sympathize with them in their problems; share their feelings of pleasure in life; say, when you feel it, "Gee, Mom, I love you!" or "Dad, I may not act that way a lot of the time, but I really do love you," or whatever words come easily to you. You may even accompany the words with a hug. That sort of behavior means a lot to parents, and some parents feel quite starved for it. (Of course, there are many families where the open expression of love by words or actions just doesn't happen, and if it suddenly did it might seem fake. And yet in most such families the feeling of being supported and loved is there, underneath.)

If you really feel unloved by your parents most of the time, try to work up the courage to tell them, not in anger, not in a time of crisis, but when you can talk about it calmly. It may be that your parents are so concerned with bringing you up right that they spend all their time criticizing you or punishing you and aren't aware how hatefully they are coming on to you. If you're to live well together, they should be aware of this. The chances are they'll be very surprised to know that you feel unloved and will change their ways a bit. But you, for your part, have got to remember that punishment or criticism doesn't mean the withdrawal of love. If your parents didn't care about you, didn't love you, they wouldn't be so concerned to have you grow up successfully and well.

And what about teachers? Do you have to love them to live well with them? No, you don't. Teachers need respect— or the appearance of it. They need to feel that they are helping you learn. They enjoy very much a feeling that you like them and enjoy them and the subjects and skills they teach you. But they are not parents, and a school isn't a family. Now and then you may really love a teacher and get a tremendous amount of emotional help and support. But even with such teachers, you need to wean yourself from them because they are not family, and next year they'll have a new set of students in whom they'll invest their skills, efforts, and caring. However, while you have a given teacher, do try to find ways to help and encourage him or her. Teachers enjoy **praise** just as much as you do, even though, in their professional way, they may not make you aware of it.

lying   see blaming; cheating; honesty

male-female behavior   see sex roles

manners

Manners are rules of conduct, the proper and polite ways to behave. Certainly, good manners, polite conduct, make the social machinery at home and at school run more smoothly. There are two sorts of good manners: those on the surface and those more deeply rooted.

Surface manners are a great help. For example: Say hi

to people when you meet or pass by them. Call them by name. Say "May I . . . ?" instead of "I'm gonna . . . !"

When you ask for something say "Please," and when you receive something, even if you didn't want it, say "Thanks." Don't borrow anything without asking first and getting permission. Be at least moderately clean and neat. Don't offend people by smelling bad.

At home, keep your room neat or at least close the door. Don't leave your things lying around.

Don't annoy people by loud talk or music when they need quiet. Share time on TV and telephone. Use good table manners.

At school, look at teachers (or take notes) when they talk. Never yawn conspicuously. Be prepared with needed equipment. Take your seat promptly and stop talking when the teacher calls the class to order.

Put things away, especially books and materials needed by other people. Don't start packing up before class is dismissed or the bell has rung. If you're late, enter quietly and explain later. Raise your hand and be recognized before speaking (unless the teacher specifically doesn't require this).

Having read this list, do you feel like exclaiming, "What a bore!" Well, good manners may be a bore, but they sure do make life pleasanter for most people, and they leave time and thought for more important things.

These are all surface manners. There's a deeper form of good manners, and that involves behaving in a way that really takes into consideration what other people—parents, teachers—need and then trying to provide it. This means you have to be alert to how people are feeling. If they're discouraged, you encourage them; if they're overworked, you offer to do a job for them; if they're happy and jolly, you enjoy being funny and laughing too; if they've worked hard and done a good job and don't feel recognized for it, you praise them. This deeper form of good manners is even more important than surface manners, and it's harder to manage. But both forms are important.

One word of caution: Some people are so correct and

mistakes

polite and mannerly with each other on the surface that they never reveal to others how they are really feeling underneath. To live well with people we need not only the easing that good manners bring but also ways to know each other's deepest feelings and needs so we can share them and help deal with them. Don't let surface good manners entirely shut people off from your real self.

marks *see* grades

mistakes

One of the things that makes life difficult is the mistakes teenagers make, and parents make, and teachers make. But since we are all human, we're all going to go on making mistakes. The poet Alexander Pope wrote, "To err is human, to forgive, divine."

What can you do about the mistakes you make? First, unless you can correct them all by yourself and undo the damage without anyone's knowing, admit you made a mistake and take the consequences. Don't deny it. Say "I'm sorry" if the mistake harmed others. Ask for advice on how to avoid the mistake in the future. It also is comforting to others if you make it known that you really want to be told if you make a mistake, so you can learn from it.

If parents or teachers make a mistake, avoid the temptation to say, in effect, "Aha! *You* made a mistake." However, unless it's a very minor matter, don't just let the mistake pass. Instead, you can say something like, "Mom, may I tell you something?" or, with a teacher, raise your hand and suggest, maybe in question form, "Does that equation really come out right?"

I know a teacher who really wants his classes to be alert. He challenges them to point out mistakes he makes, and he makes at least two in each class on purpose, after telling his students he'll do it. This keeps things lively. (Also it saves him embarrassment if he does something wrong without knowing it!) Of course, if no one notices a mistake, he points it out before the end of class so that the error will not be learned as truth.

One of the best classrooms I ever was in had a large sign over the chalkboard in front of the room: IT'S SAFE TO MAKE A MISTAKE IN THIS ROOM. A great idea, because from risking error, we learn. However, the sign continued: BUT MORE TO YOUR CREDIT TO MAKE A DIFFERENT ONE EACH TIME.

That would be a good motto for any class or home. We learn together.

money

Money is a major cause of conflict in many families. Arguments about it are actually one of the main causes of divorce. And one of the things parents say they worry most about is whether or not their children will learn **responsibility** in the ways they spend money. Will they learn "the value of a dollar"? When they leave home, will they be able to take care of themselves? Obviously, with these questions in the minds of many parents, if you and your parents are going to live well together, you'll probably need to spend some time considering money.

One of the best ways to learn to use money responsibly and intelligently is to have some to use. This is a good reason to give children **allowances,** to spend or save as they see fit. Earning money from **jobs** (not **chores**) is also a very good way to learn about its importance and management.

To develop skills in managing money, learn how to make a budget, an estimate of how much money you will need for various items—books, travel, meals outside the home, clothes, entertainment, presents, gifts to charity, saving up for a desired special item (TV set, phone, cycle, car, musical instrument). Then keep a record of your expenses to see how close they come to the estimate.

Open and maintain a savings or checking account.

Get a loan for a special need and plan how to repay it. (If you borrow from your parents, be sure you both agree that it's a loan, not a gift, and that the amount is written down along with a schedule for repayment.) *Note:* I'm not saying that parents shouldn't make gifts to their children. It's wonderful to receive a gift freely given and to express thanks for it. But it's not good for relationships if you keep nagging for a gift. It's not good either if you fail to repay a loan which then, in a way very annoying to parents, becomes a grudging gift.

Family Checkbook

This is not a game, but it is a serious, useful, and educational activity. Arrange with your mother or father actually to keep the family checkbook for a period of time. That is, after a period of careful instruction, you make out the checks for paying the family bills, you enter the deposits into the account, and you keep the balance. Of course, it will have to be a parent who actually signs the checks and who inspects the job to be sure it's done right, but you learn all about the process and also get a clear idea of the state of the family's finances. Once you've learned the job, you can be a big help to your parents by taking it over when necessary. Also, it's very good training for future jobs you may hold, or for having your own checking account later.

The common teenage practice of unscheduled asking, begging, or pleading for money to pay for some unexpected expense is not a good way to strengthen relationships with parents. The parents tend to feel angry if they have to give and guilty if they decide to refuse. They also may feel that you ought to learn to plan better. And you may tend to feel like a plotter—"I'll get him when he's in a good mood" or "I'll be *very* nice to her for a few days and then . . . " It's much better, if you're into the pattern of running to your parents for emergency funds, to find a time when there's no specific money emergency at hand and then to discuss: (1) your needs, (2) your resources, (3) the family's resources, and (4) how to plan to meet your needs.

If your family is really hard up for money to meet its basic expenses, you can make a wonderful contribution by getting a job and voluntarily turning over to your parents a good part of what you earn. Discuss this in advance, so your parents will understand what you plan to do. Or you can use your earnings to meet more and more of your own expenses, even to the point of being able to say that you no longer need an allowance. Be sure, though, that the demands of the job don't interfere with your schoolwork.

Is it a good idea for you to know what the financial resources of your family are? Should you know such things as how much your parents earn, what savings and other income they have, how much the house is worth, and what insurance policies they have? By the time people are teenagers, most of them are ready to understand and deal with this information, and it will help to make them more intelligent participants in family affairs. However, many—perhaps most—parents feel their finances are confidential, and they fear that if their children have too much information, it may get spread around. It's important for you to understand and respect this fear. Often it is based on fact. People, teenage or not, find it difficult not to tell too much. But if you are trustworthy, it can increase family harmony and understanding for you and your parents to share financial information. At least it's a good question to discuss.

As you gain skill in planning for the earning and spending of money, you may be useful to teachers by offering to take responsibility for the financial aspects of class and school projects—fund-raising campaigns, service projects, class trips, and so forth. Some teachers and administrators will be very grateful for help. So, if you have the time and interest, talk it over at school.

moods

A mood is a state of mind, and what our state of mind is affects what we do and how we treat people. Therefore, if you are aware of the mood that your parents or your teachers are in, you will probably be better able to get through each day with them. Also, if you're aware of your own moods, and allow for them, you may be easier to live with. The teenage years are recognized as a period of quick swings of mood, probably because most teenagers *music*   82

have a lot on their minds all at the same time: school, friends, popularity, sex, career, appearance, clothes, ideals—how life is going to come out, if at all. Will you be a flop or a freak or a super-success? It's normal for anybody to feel moody.

What are some moods? We speak of being in a bad mood, a grouchy mood, a happy mood, a sentimental mood, a prickly mood, a goofy mood, a worried mood, a quiet mood, a stormy mood, a dark mood, an angry mood, a carefree mood, a reckless mood, a depressed mood—you can add to the list. It is helpful sometimes to say straight out, "I'm in a lousy mood tonight. I don't know why. Don't worry about it." Or, before you ask a teacher or parent a difficult question or for some kind of help or privilege, it can be useful to ask first, "What sort of mood are you in?" If you are alert to signs (see **tone of voice; body language**), you may not even have to ask.

Mood Warnings

In one family, the mother keeps a mood-announcement place on the kitchen bulletin board and thumbtacks on it signs like WATCH OUT, BAD MOOD; FEEL FREE, GOOD MOOD; or DANGER! FEELING MAD. Some teachers do the same thing by writing on the chalkboard if they feel extra hard-pressed. It's one of the realities of life students need to learn to adjust to.

However, the best thing you can do is try to be sensitive to the moods of parents and teachers and act accordingly. See also **feelings.**

motivation   see **goals**

music

In some families, differing tastes in music cause nearly violent **conflicts.** You like rock, your parents like classical, neither of you can stand Country and Western, so you settle for Muzak or silence, whatever the situation may be. People have a right to silence where they live, so if you can't agree on what kinds of musical noises you enjoy, get earphones or a Walkman. Nothing can be more annoying to parents than to hear coming from your room (where you're supposed to be doing your homework) some kind of musical whomping when they're trying to read or enjoy a TV program. They find it hard to understand that, as one girl put it, "I've got to have something to keep my mind on while I'm doing my homework." More accurately, for many people it does help to have some sort of so-called white noise to shut out the distractions of other family activities, and the more mindless the music the better.

By the way, a few families find that a wonderful way to enjoy each other's company is to perform music together, even badly.

negotiating

When people or organizations negotiate, they talk and discuss problems or **conflicts**, put forth their opinions and their needs, and keep working at the matter until they reach a settlement, an agreement. The alternative to negotiation is either fighting (going on strike) or giving in and accepting, happily or unhappily, what the other side demands. Fortunately, in almost all families there's a lot of negotiation—working things out to the best interests of all.

There's no negotiating with a small baby. The baby cries and complains when it doesn't get what it needs, and the parents pretty well have to give in—one hopes with love, hugs, and smiles. With small children, quite often there's not much negotiating, although probably there should be. Many children, once they understand speech, are simply required to do what must be done and to do it "the way it's s'posed to be."

But by the time you're a teenager, negotiation becomes essential because you're growing up, you have a mind of your own, and you're getting ready in a few years to become independent. Unfortunately, many parents fail to realize that they should move gradually from **orders** to negotiation and working things out. If they don't switch, it may mean that their children revolt, or they remain obedient children who don't mature well, or they move more and more outside the family where they can develop independence despite their parents.

If you feel there's not enough negotiation of problems going on in your family, it might be a good start to read aloud together the first three paragraphs of this topic, discuss them, and then make a tentative list of matters that might be negotiated. Some of the advantages of negotiation are: It requires you and your parents to think. (It was Mark Twain who said that the brain is the least used part of the human body.) It gives choices and bargaining, and to have to make choices and bargain is a good way to grow up and become mature. The solutions reached by negotiation usually last longer and are more acceptable than those that are dictated or arrived at only after nagging till someone gives up. It involves give-and-take and talking, which help everyone involved understand one another better. It helps prepare your parents for *your* adulthood.

So, if there are some important problems to be worked out at home, why not suggest, "Let's negotiate"? Subjects might include **rules, homework,** use of **TV** and **telephone, chores, jobs,** what to have for meals, **allowances, parties, hours,** and so forth. Remember, though, that parents and teenagers don't negotiate as equals. Your parents are basically responsible for you and for the family until you reach adulthood.

What about negotiation at school? Again, you can't negotiate with teachers as equals. Teachers have to be in charge, even though the more responsibility they can delegate to you the better. However, on such matters as schedules of tests, amount of homework, and types of classroom activities, negotiation can be very educational, and it can help keep teachers in touch with the lives of students. Thus you can ask for—but you'd better not demand—negotiation.

normalcy

One of the worst put-downs in the English language can be the word *normal*. "It's not normal, what you're doing!"

(Translation: "You're strange and peculiar, and I don't like you.") One of the things many teenagers worry about is "Am I normal?"

Most of us aren't utterly normal, thank heavens. Life would be very dull if we were. *Normal* does not mean *good* or *right* or *ideal* or *desirable*. It means "according to the norm," the middle, the average. One could say that if you have very high intelligence or unusual talents in academic subjects, the arts, or sports, you are not normal. You're blessedly above normal; you're original.

Of course, there are kinds of behavior that are not normal—they're *abnormal,* just as a body temperature of well above 98.6 degrees Fahrenheit is not normal; it's a sign that there's something wrong with you. If a person tries to commit **suicide,** that's not normal; if a person tries to starve to death, that's not normal; if a person refuses to talk to anyone, or talks compulsively and won't stop, that's not normal. These conditions need expert treatment. But people who are their original selves, even if everybody doesn't agree with them, are not abnormal. They're what the world needs more of, and they'll find their creative place in it.

obstacles *see* goals

openness

Some people say quite simply that if only parents and children were more open with each other, family life would improve. Probably this is true, but it's certainly not simple. If we were open, if we expressed ourselves freely within the family, if we had no **secrets,** it's true that we would have the possibility of understanding each other better. We'd know how other people felt and what was happening to them, and we would therefore be able to be more considerate of them.

However, it would be a disaster for relationships if we were totally open. We sometimes have **feelings** that are much better not expressed. For example, if for a moment you hate your father or wish your mother would go away and stay away, or think you'd rather live in another family, or that everybody would be happier, including you, if you were dead, it certainly wouldn't be a good idea to say all these things every time you felt them. And yet they are perfectly normal ways to feel—from time to time. The feelings pass. Wouldn't it be awful if you had an electronic news announcer running across your forehead so that anyone could read the state of your feelings as you had them? We keep many of our feelings to ourselves. There's no need to feel guilty about it.

Also, you don't have to tell your parents everything that happens to you either, or everything that you've done, good or bad. If you did, it would be too much of a burden for them. And if your father and mother told you all their worries and problems and actions, it would be too much of a burden for you. We all have a right to privacy and a need for it, and it's no fun to have people prying into our thoughts and actions.

Another point is that you are probably more open than you think you are. **Body language** and **tone of voice** reveal quite a lot of what you're feeling even though you don't directly say it. The same goes for your parents.

Here are a few other points about openness. Language—**words**—is a very useful form of openness, and if you want to avoid being misunderstood, saying directly how you feel can be a great help. Sometimes it's helpful to ask your parents how they feel, or how their day went, or what their problems are. They may be glad to have an opportunity to be open with you about these things. **Arguments** and **fights** and **yelling** are forms of openness too. They reveal what people feel strongly about. They can let you know when you're trespassing where you shouldn't. Probably families would be happier if they argued, fought, and yelled less, but I'm not sure.

Openness is better than closing yourself in silence and just sulking—at least usually it is. Now and then people should have the right to a good sulk! It, too, is a form of **communication**. But it's hard to take much of it from other people, so don't be an over-sulker.

With teachers, who are responsible for scores of students and can't be in tune with each of them all the time, it's wise to be careful about when to be open. You'll have many feelings about the subjects taught and about teachers personally that are better left unsaid, except for those that are encouraging. However, if there are really important things that are bothering people and that you think teachers might be able to do something about, it's good to figure out a good time and way to tell them. This might have to do with such matters as amount of homework, scheduling of tests, an explanation that wasn't clear. It shouldn't have to do with the teacher's personality or appearance, or details of the teacher's family life.

orders

If you get an order or a command from a parent or teacher to do something or to stop doing something, you'd better obey. When people who have some authority over you actually order you, they almost certainly mean it, and if you don't obey it's not going to be easy to live with them. However, families and schools are not armies, which are run on the basis of orders and unquestioning obedience. If there is a lot of ordering around in your family, maybe you need to say, with a wry smile, something like, "I didn't realize this was the army. But, anyway, yes, *sir!*" That ought to open the way to talking about the whole situation sometime.

Try not to let simple ordering and obeying get to be a habit in the family. In the long run, unless it's done on a semi-humorous basis and by agreement, it's a poor way to live together. Simple obedience of orders does not teach you to think for yourself or to be independent and self-sufficient. This would be a very good subject for discussion.

School is somewhat different. Teachers, even when there's no fire drill, may sometimes need to give orders, or at least to tell students what to do and expect them to do it without question. This can be especially true during the first few days of the school year when systems and procedures are being established. But it's much better if "instructions" are given, not orders. Again, after you've gotten to know your teachers pretty well, this might make a good subject for discussion. "Is order-obeying educational?" could be the question. But be sure to pose it respectfully!

As for you, a teenager, it is never appropriate for you to give an order to a parent or a teacher. It's much better to make requests. Preface them with "Would you mind if...?" or "Could I suggest that...?" and end the request with "please."

parent-teacher conferences

You have one life, but in a way it's divided into two parts: life at home and life at school. (Of course, there's also life outside of home and outside of school, which becomes a larger and larger slice of life as you go through your teens.) It's totally unrealistic to expect that your parents should know all about school or your teachers know all about home, but if you're having any kind of serious problem, especially at school, it's often good if both your parents and teachers know about it. This is the reason for parent-teacher conferences. Some teenagers worry that a conference, especially if it's arranged at the special request of parents or of a teacher and not just routine, may be a kind of plot of the powers against them. This isn't true, but it's an understandable feeling. Take it from someone who's been through hundreds of parent-teacher conferences: their purpose is to help you do better at school, perhaps also at home, and eventually in life. You can be grateful that parents and teachers are taking time to help see together those two parts of your life.

What can you do to make parent-teacher conferences more useful? If you know there's to be a conference, talk over with your parents in advance what you think they ought to discuss with the teacher. After all, it's your life. You might try to have a word with the teacher, too, but only if you think there's something the teacher might not hear from your parents and really needs to know. And few teachers have time to confer with each pupil before a parent conference. But be careful not to discuss with teachers matters that your parents consider confidential. If you think there are ways in which your parents and your teachers are—probably unintentionally—working against each other, or on the basis of different ideas about the right kind of education for you, take the initiative and suggest a conference. Tell your parents, and maybe the teacher, why you are suggesting it. (Even the act of telling might improve the situation.) After the conference, be sure to ask your parents what went on and what they learned or said that might help you. Are there things you should be doing differently?

My conviction is that in most cases it is much better if you yourself are in on the conference. That is, it would be a parent-teacher-student conference. It's your life they're talking about. What they say you probably ought to hear. As a teenager, you're old enough to hear it. And, since you know quite a lot about your life, there are probably things you can explain to both parents and teachers that will enable them to live better with you, and you with them, and that will improve your education. So, if you feel OK about it, ask to be a participant in the conference. At least, then people won't have to spend time afterward telling you what happened. You were there. Also, it may be a wonderful way to open up subjects for good discussion with your parents later.

parties

Parties at the homes of teenagers can be a great source of friction and conflict between parent and child. If you're a social person and have been to some parties, you probably know this already. Also, teenagers do get into trouble at parties (fights, drunkenness, experimentation with drugs, having sex, crashing, not going home on time, and so forth), so the subject is a serious one and the conflicts aren't just based on imagination. Obviously, if there are going to be parties, there must be some **rules** and regulations to avoid trouble and yet to let people have fun. And, don't forget, your parents may be legally responsible if they allow you to have a party at their house and someone gets into serious trouble as a result of what goes on.

Here are some suggestions about teenage parties. It's a good idea for you to go over them with your parents, well in advance of having a party at your house or even in advance of your going to a party at someone else's house.

Plan the party together. You know what sorts of things your friends will enjoy doing; your parents know the rules of your house and that they are responsible even though it's mostly your party. Once you've done some planning with your own parents, it can be useful to get together with a couple of your friends who are coming and also their parents, so there will be a group of people of both generations who know what the arrangements are and can help make things go well. (This would be for a largish party, maybe eight or more people. If only five or six people are coming, it doesn't have to be such a big deal.)

A party should have a definite guest list, names written down. "Open houses" are invitations for disaster because no one feels responsible, and because friends may bring friends that you don't even know, or word gets around and all sorts of people come. The guest list should be known, and you and your parents must be prepared to stick to it and politely but firmly turn away people not on the list, no matter how nice and friendly they are. In other words, no crashing. Parents should be at or near the door to greet guests by name when they arrive and to say good night and thanks when they leave. This can be a friendly, welcoming exchange, and it also lets the guests know whose house they are in—a house belonging to real human beings who talk and smile and think!

Unlike adult parties, teenage parties must have definite hours for starting and ending, and you should expect people to depart at the end. If no one comes to pick them up, use the telephone or get your parents to do so.

A teenage party needs adult chaperons—adults who are there and responsible. Often it's pleasanter for the chaperons if they can be more than just your two parents, so they can enjoy themselves together and not always be right in there with the kids. But they should circulate from time to time. They can do this easily if they help with things like passing the food. Also parties are best if there are a number of activities people can engage in, not just sitting around and listening to music. Plan some games, or at least have them available. And, of course, consuming food and soft drinks is a great activity. Provide food—maybe your friends can share in this job.

There must be a clear understanding about **smoking, alcohol, and drugs.** Certainly, no drugs or alcoholic beverages—even beer—should be allowed. Most, probably all, of those attending are under the legal drinking age, so it is a criminal act to allow drinking in the house at a party. And the use of drugs is illegal at any age. Smoking is a less clear situation. There's no law against smoking at any age, and yet many people are convinced—rightly—that smoking is a very unhealthy activity. If smoking is allowed at a party, some of your guests are going to feel under pressure to smoke, even though they really don't want to. Also, the nonsmokers will find themselves inhaling smoky air—suffering from "passive smoking," which is also bad for the health. My view is that smoking should be forbidden at teenage parties (even if habit-ridden adults smoke in another room!). At any rate, this is a question you and your parents must work out together ahead of time and enforce your agreement.

It should be understood which parts of the house are open to party guests and which parts are not. Upstairs rooms and bedrooms should be off limits. (You can even post a few little OFF LIMITS signs.) There should be an agreement about light: probably dim (that makes people's complexions look better), but no dark rooms. It should be understood that once people arrive at a party, they stay. No leaving and coming back or wandering around the neighborhood. In-and-out parties are too likely to allow people to go out and have an illegal drink and then come back.

From these ideas, you can figure out what the understandings with your parents should be when you go to someone else's party. Basically, your parents should know where you're going, including the phone number of the place; how you're going to get there; what time the party starts and ends; and how you're getting home. (See **transportation**.) Also, when you go to a party, if you want to get along well with your friends' parents, look over the suggestions above and apply them to yourself. Further, you will be greatly appreciated by the teenage host and his or her parents if you offer to help with food, games, and generally having a good time.

Some schools organize parties for classes or groups. The same sorts of suggestions apply to school parties as to home parties, except that the group of attenders is likely to be considerably larger. A party at school is basically the school's responsibility, even though most of the jobs of organizing it and running it will be delegated to students and parents—perhaps members of the PTA. You can be a great strengthener if you offer to help and even offer up your parents to help chaperon—getting their consent first, of course.

peer pressure

As you grow from childhood to adulthood—that is, through adolescence—you become less and less dependent upon your parents and more and more involved with and related to people of your own age group, your peers. Keep in mind that it may be quite difficult for your parents to accept this shifting of your life center. (On the other hand, there are many parents who welcome it and just love the idea of your getting to be more and more on your own.)

When you feel that your peers are strongly influencing you in certain ways (say, your **appearance,** whether you begin **smoking,** what **hours** you keep, what kinds of **music** you like, what your attitude toward school is, and so forth), that's called *peer pressure.* Adults feel peer pressure too. And peer pressure isn't all bad. It's good to be sensitive to what "the group" likes and how to get along with the group. But it's also good to be your own person, with your own principles and beliefs, many of which you have learned from your family. (I once asked over 400 teenagers whether they generally approved of the moral and social standards of their families. Ninety percent replied *yes*.)

One of your interesting tasks is to interpret to your parents what your peers are thinking and feeling and to keep your peers in touch with what your parents think and feel.

At school, there may be special problems, and they can affect how successfully you get along with teachers. If the peer culture (some people even describe teenagers together as "tribal") respects doing well at school as "in" and "with it," you are fortunate. If, as seems to be the case in many schools, the "tribe" opposes—or at least does not support—those who work hard and are academically ambitious, then you have to be your own person and stand up for what's important to you. It can be useful to talk with some of your teachers about this. They will see the importance of the conflict, and they will get satisfaction from helping you to do your best.

One further suggestion: Be careful not to be taken in by the idea that "everybody's doing it"—and therefore you'd better get with it and do it too. The "it" that everybody's doing may refer to having sex, drinking, smoking, trying drugs, or just goofing off. Some of your peers who are confident and bold, who may have physically matured quite early, and who seem to be very "in" and popular, are so ready to talk big that people who are less big-time hesitate to speak up. Never mind; have courage. In the end you all will mature physically, and the early bloomers don't do any better in the long run than the late ones. In fact, many who, as teenagers, feel out of the tribe, are original thinkers, strongly ambitious, and are developing qualities more important than **popularity** at the moment. In many cases, they will go far.

This is a good subject to discuss with parents and teachers, because the "everybody's doing it" idea can be very distressing to them.

pets

Sometimes under the pressures of teenage life it seems as if your dog or your cat is the only creature that loves you. As an eight-year-old boy wrote in an essay on *What My Dog Means to Me,* "My dog means somebody nice and quiet to be with. He does not say 'Do' like my mother, or 'Don't' like my father, or 'Stop' like my big brother. My dog Spot and I sit together quietly, and I like him and he likes me."

If you really *need* a pet, talk it over with your parents. Be sure that the need doesn't blind you to the effects of the pet on others in your family, who may be worried by hairs, smells, and noises, not to mention feeding and walking the pet when you are late getting home.

please and thanks

This little entry is just to remind you of an obvious, easy truth. When you want something, the old magic word "Please" is likely to open the way and keep parents and teachers feeling good, and the other magic word, "Thanks!"—or even, "Gee, thanks very much!"—will make them glad they did whatever you wanted.

politeness *see* manners

popularity

There are so many attractive, able teenagers who are miserable because they feel they aren't popular that I'm convinced that popularity usually isn't worth the struggle. Sure, if it happens easily, it's fun to be liked by a lot of people and to be in with the group, but not if you have to act phony or do things you really don't believe in or enjoy. Why bother? All we really need, unless we're running for office, is a few good **friends.**

Another thing about the struggle for popularity is that it may tend to spoil your relationship with your parents and teachers. If you find yourself acting like a wise guy or spending so much time with the group that you're doing poorly in your schoolwork or not doing your chores at home or spending some time with your parents, again, probably popularity isn't worth it.

If you feel really unpopular—disliked by your age group—find a good, relaxed time and ask a friend, or even a popular, secure person who isn't a friend, "Why don't people seem to like me? Are there things I should do or stop doing? I *really* want to know, so please tell me the truth." A question like that can gain you respect from the person you ask, and you may find out some useful things.

Feeling unpopular can make you grouchy and hard to live with, not only for your classmates but also for your parents and teachers. You might try asking your parents—one or both of them, however you feel most comfortable—why you feel unpopular. Or ask a teacher you trust, and who knows what's going on, the same question. You may get some good, specific suggestions about how you act, how you dress, how you spend your time, and what you might do to develop friends. Furthermore, sharing problems with your parents and a couple of teachers helps you to live better with them, too.

Sometime, suggest to, say, an English teacher that a good subject for the class to write about and discuss is "What Makes People Popular?" or "How Important Is It to Be Popular?" An assignment and discussion like this produces lots of good ideas and makes people more sensitive to each other.

If there are ways that teachers or parents are treating you that you think are making people dislike you, tell them so. Maybe a teacher calls on you too much, or makes you seem like a **teacher's pet,** or makes fun of you (maybe without even realizing it), or assigns you to the wrong discussion group. Or maybe your parents won't let you fit the customs of your group in matters like **hours, parties,** and so forth, even when those customs are not harmful, or maybe they don't treat your friends nicely, or whatever—well, find a time to tell them and discuss the problem.

If you have no problems with popularity but know someone who does, try to help that person just as you might want to be helped. Invite the person over to your house, or to sit with you at lunch, or to join your group in class. It can be a godsend to someone who is suffering from feeling disliked.

Last, back to you, if you're not popular and find it hard to make friends, watch *yourself*. Act friendly, no matter what; don't moan and groan; find an interest or activity that you can share with others; and remember, things will almost certainly change (even though in your misery you may find it hard to believe). *See also* **normalcy; peer pressure.**

praise

Everybody in the world likes to be praised for things they do well, and feeling approved makes us easier to live with. But often we are so busy with our own lives that we forget this. People work hard, do well, help make things better, and we seldom remember to say, "Gee, that was a great job you did!" or "I really enjoy the way you teach this class," or "Dad, the way you helped me understand that math problem was super; you should be a teacher," or "You really look great today," or "That was the best meal anybody could cook!" (not "the best meal we've had in a long time"!).

Parents really love it when their children praise them, and it's hard for teenagers to remember this. If parents have to ask, "Did you like the way I [whatever it was]" it's not nearly as rewarding as if you say on your own, "I really liked the way you . . . " Shakespeare expressed the negative side of the matter in his play *King Lear* when he wrote, "How sharper than a serpent's tooth it is/To have a thankless child!"—a child who never expresses appreciation.

One caution about praise: Be sure it's honest. Don't praise somebody for a good job when it really wasn't. (Also, if you know *you* did a good job, tell yourself! Or you can even say something like, "Mom, am I doing my weekend chores OK?" If you are, she'll probably say so.)

Strength-O-Grams

Often we spend so much time saying what's wrong with our friends, or what weaknesses they need to improve, that we don't ever share our strengths. In this activity, a small group of people (all the family; five or so classmates seated in a small circle) each writes a Strength-O-Gram (brief, like a telegram) to the person on the left. The Strength-O-Gram states a strength that the other person has. For example: *Janey. You always are helpful in explaining how to get started on a math problem if people ask you.* Or: *Kevin. Just having you smile at a person across the table at meals makes that person feel great.* Then the Strength-O-Gram is passed to Janey or Kevin, and they read it silently and then aloud to the whole group.

Trade-lasts

One large family of parents, children, and grandchildren I know uses this game to keep everyone encouraged and happy. When a member of the family, say Norris, hears something nice about, say, his sister Carla, he says to Carla, "Trade-last!" He means that before Carla can hear what the nice thing is, she must think of something nice about him. She says it first, and then Norris gives his trade-last. Friends can use trade-lasts too.

privacy *see* your room/locker/desk

problem-solving

People who live or work together are bound to have problems. Usually, except in math, science, and carefully constructed puzzles, problems are never solved once and for all. Rather, they are dealt with, are solved for a time, and then come up again, to be dealt with again as circumstances change. This is especially true of problems concerning relationships between people and the way people behave.

The Conflict Resolution activity (*see* **conflicts**) describes

problem-solving

a definite way to solve serious problems between or among people, both at school and at home, that involves using your brain. The steps suggested are: (1) Define the problem, (2) brainstorm solutions, (3) evaluate the solutions, (4) agree on a solution, (5) commit yourself to trying the solution, and (6) meet again and discuss how the solution is working.

There are several ways that *don't* work in solving problems. You may have tried some of them. They include: (1) *Doing nothing.* Sometimes a problem will just go away, but usually it takes some thought and talk and work to make it do so. (2) *Escaping.* If the problem is at home or at school, you've got it. Trying to escape is probably futile. (3) *Rebelling.* If you just protest and refuse to help, you're probably going to make the problem worse. Furthermore, rebellion tends to make people's minds blind to reality. (4) *Lying and cheating.* These might work for a brief time and make the problem seem solved for you, but they always sow the seeds of a worse problem and make it harder to solve, because trust is gone.

A suggestion: If a parent or a teacher says "I need to see you about something" (or "about the way you've been behaving" or "about a problem"), try starting off your discussion by saying something like, "I've been thinking about things. May I tell you what I think you want to see me about?" This will show the parent or the teacher that you *have* been thinking, a good sign, and that you take the matter seriously. It also will help remove any anger or hostility there may be. Then, after you say what you think the problem is, if you have figured it out right, you can say, "Well, I've also been thinking what I can do about it," and go ahead and suggest how you might help solve the problem.

This method often works. However, sometimes parents and teachers are all set for the meeting and *they tell you!* They scold ("It's really bad the way you [whatever it is]," they preach ("Here's what I expect you to do"), and they threaten punishment ("Here's what's going to happen if you don't do it"). The trouble with this pattern is that it doesn't give you a chance to think about your behavior. Well, OK, listen. And then say, "Well, I hear you. Can I tell what I've thought of?"

If you persist in thinking about things and about what you might do to improve the situation, you may find a gradual but dramatic improvement in the ways you and your parents and teachers live together. See also negotiating.

promises

Occasionally, when people really want to commit themselves to something, they say, "I promise to . . ." Promises are useful blocks on which to build good relationships. But promises should not be made lightly, so think carefully and take your time before you say "I promise." Sometimes a parent or teacher will say, "Now I want you to promise me never to . . ." or "always to . . ." Should you make the promise? My advice is not to promise unless you are sure. You could reply (in school, raising your hand first!), "A promise is a serious thing. I just want to be sure I understand what we're promising." This may lead to some good discussion.

Sometimes you make a promise and then things change and you no longer feel it's right or even possible to do what you promised. For example, you promised to come home from school within an hour of the last scheduled activity. Now you find that a lot of unscheduled, very interesting things are happening between the end of school and suppertime. There's good conversation around the buildings or down at the corner drugstore or at people's houses. Lots of friendships are being made—it's where the action is. You really don't want to miss out on all this. What to do? Don't break your promise. Explain the situation to your parents and say that you have to withdraw your promise.

Or take another example. You promised not to smoke. But things have changed, and a lot of your friends smoke, and you want to see what it's like. Explain this to your parents and say you're going to try it. Their arguments about the health hazards still stand, they're still against smoking, and they have the right to forbid smoking in their house. But still you want to try it. Again explain, and then withdraw your promise. Maybe you'll want to promise to report to your parents later on how it went, whether you enjoy smoking, and what you intend to do in the future. That way, you keep communications open.

To sum up: Think carefully before promising. If you make a promise, stick by it. And if you need to withdraw a promise, explain why and talk about it.

protesting

To protest means to make a definite objection or complaint. Often it goes along with a refusal to cooperate, a refusal to do something, or a refusal to accept what somebody else does or says. "I protest!" is strong language, and it arouses resistance on the part of the person the protest is made to. Sometimes a protest can get attention and remedial action ("I protest your going into my room like that"; "I protest being kept after school when I've done nothing wrong"). But more often it only arouses resistance and determination not to give in. Usually, it's much better to say something like "May I ask a question about that?" or "I've got a suggestion—would you like to hear it?" or "I need to explain something that I feel very strongly about, OK?"

psychologist/psychiatrist see help

punishment

If people do what they shouldn't do, often they get punished. And when they know they'll be punished, they stop doing the bad thing. With small children, punishment is often simple and effective. But more effective than punishment is *showing* people what the right way to behave is and *explaining* why the bad behavior is bad. Even better, when a person is old enough to think, is to ask him or her to *figure out* why behavior is bad and what kind of behavior would be better. (*See also* **rewards**.)

By the time you're a teenager you're probably too old to be helped much by direct punishment, especially physical punishment. If you are punished by parents or teachers, you could say, "Please tell me how this is going to improve my behavior." But if you really have done something wrong (stayed out late, willfully disobeyed your parents or teacher, damaged some property, stolen or cheated, copied someone else's work, knowingly broken a school rule) you "deserve" to be punished and should take your punishment and try to learn from it.

If you have a chance, say something like, "OK, I know I shouldn't have done [whatever it was], and I ought to be punished. How about if I suggest a punishment that I think will make me behave better?" And then, if you're given a chance, suggest a punishment that "fits the crime." Here are some examples. *Crime:* Stayed out later than allowed. *Punishment:* Be grounded for a week and do some extra chores during the grounded time. *Crime:* Cheated on a test. *Punishment:* Get a failing grade on the test, write a thoughtful essay on the causes and consequences of cheating, and be given a chance to take the test again, just to prove that you know the material. *Crime:* Carelessly—or willfully—broke or damaged some object or property at home or at school. *Punishment:* Either repair what you damaged or pay to have it repaired, earning the money to do so if you haven't got it, plus repairing or improving some other objects or property to compensate for the trouble you have caused. A fine example, in fun, is the sign on a crocodile pit in a game park in the African country of Kenya. It reads, VISITORS WHO THROW REFUSE INTO THE CROCODILE PIT WILL BE ASKED TO RETRIEVE IT.

Crime and Punishment

With a group of people, have each one write on an index card a "crime," one at home or one at school. Then exchange cards and have another person write a punishment that will "fit the crime"—that is, will be just, useful, and likely to prevent another crime. Then read the cards aloud and discuss them.

Remember, in schools there is usually a complex system of **rules** and of punishments for breaking them. These may seem rigid and unhelpful to you, or even unfair, but your best policy, if you want to get on well, is to accept the system, take the punishments, obey the rules—and then, when it's all over, find an opportunity to discuss how the system might be improved. Prepare yourself with some ideas (maybe based on discussion with friends, parents, a teacher), so that you'll have some intelligent suggestions to make.

put-downs

People of any age are easier to live with if they feel good about themselves. Getting in the habit of putting people down, even in small ways, makes life harder at home and at school. Telling people, directly or indirectly, that they are stupid, ugly, insensitive, lazy, or just not very important is damaging, so resist the temptation to do it. Never say, in a complaining or negative way, "You always [whatever it is]" or "You never . . . " or "You know perfectly well that . . . " or "I've already *told* you about . . . " or "Aren't you ever going to learn . . . ?"

The opposites of put-downs are honest **praise**, straight-out appreciation, positive feedback, or even "Great!" with a smile or a hug.

questioning

One of the characteristics of teenagers is to question things. It's a healthy habit of mind, but it can be hard to live with. A constant "Why do we have to [whatever it is]?" or "What's the use of . . . ?"—asked about well-established, reasonable **rules** and requirements—can be very trying, especially to teachers whose lives are made possible by an established system on the basis of which their schools run. It's tiresome to have to go over the same old questions month after month, year after year, even though schools should indeed explain their systems and rules if they expect to have students respect them. On the other hand, most teachers welcome good questions that lead to discussion and a questing (or seeking) for answers.

Some suggestions about questions: A question is better than **protesting** or **rebellion.** "May we discuss why we are required to [whatever it is]?" is almost always better than "I refuse to . . " or "I really protest. . . . " When you ask a question, especially one about routines or requirements at school or home, be careful about your **tone of voice.** Avoid a complaining or whining tone. Ask politely, but directly, showing that you really want to know. Don't ask too many questions too often. Think first, then question. And be sensitive to the **moods** of people whom you are going to question. When a parent is grouchy or hurried or depressed or jittery, it's not a good time to ask a "Why do we have to . . . ?" question. Better to say, "OK, Mom, how can I help? I've got a little extra time."

reading

Some people have difficulty with reading because they think there is only one way to do it: Sit down, start at the beginning, read steadily to the end, and then stop. Actually, there are at least five types of reading: (1) *skimming*, for a general overview of the material or to find specific items of information; (2) rapid, relaxed *pleasure reading*, to enjoy a story or an account of something you're interested in; (3) *close, active reading*, for mastery, used with textbooks, encyclopedias, and other materials from which you must learn the main facts and ideas; (4) *word-for-word reading*, perhaps aloud (or aloud inside your mind, saying each word silently), for directions or for math and science problems; and (5) *poetry reading* (and perhaps plays), best done aloud, for meaning, images, feelings, and sound. Before you start something, think about what kind of reading it requires.

If you are not a good reader, tell your teacher or your guidance counselor and ask for special instruction. Most schools provide it. The earlier it comes, the better. At school, try carrying a good book around with you to read. It's a great way to stay out of trouble.

Some people enjoy reading and read very well but hate to read aloud. If you are one of these, tell your teacher and maybe you won't have to be called on. Reading aloud is a great art and pleasure, but you can get along very well in life without it. If you've got to read aloud—say from your own writing or from a book the whole class is reading—ask the teacher to let you know in advance so you can practice a bit.

rebellion

To rebel means to resist or oppose authority, often loudly and vigorously, sometimes silently and sullenly. It's a strong word. Synonyms for rebellion are *revolution, uprising, revolt, insurrection, mutiny.* In the public events of history and the present day, rebellion is often useful, noble, and heroic, but in life at home and at school, against parents and teachers, rebellion is almost always harmful and destructive. It's quite natural to *feel* like rebelling now and then, but if you feel that way in general and over a continued period, the situation is bad and you need help—and so, probably, do your parents and teachers.

One good way to put your sense of rebellion into perspective and get yourself back on track is to write down, just for your own use, a list of rules, actions, people, and things that make you feel rebellious. Then examine the list to see whether there are parts of it you can do something about. After this you might rewrite your list with the idea of sharing it with your parents—or one of them. Often this can reduce tensions and even bring about changes.

Sometimes, though, you don't feel like writing. You're too emotionally involved. In that case, try **talking things over** with someone you trust. Just getting it off your chest can make you feel better. So can a frank reaction or advice from the listener.

If none of these things helps, try to live with your rebellious feelings for a time to see if they don't pass away. If they don't, and you feel seriously rebellious to the point that you can't live with your parents or work with your teachers except in a hostile way, ask for professional **help.**

I repeat, though, don't be too easily upset by your feelings. It's natural for teenagers to feel strongly about things, and usually rebellious feelings can be put to work to make life better. See also **protesting.**

religion

In some families, religion is a set of common beliefs and practices that bring all members together in a remarkable way, no matter how freely and frankly they may talk and argue about many of the subjects discussed in this book. In other families, some members may feel strongly religious and others strongly opposed to faith and belief. The most important thing is to respect one another's religion—or lack of religion. Also, religion can be an extremely interesting subject to discuss, provided there's no ridicule or hostility expressed, but only a search to understand and a willingness to listen and consider and deal with facts as well as faith. We need to be open, respectful, and even show a sense of **humor.**

A story I like is about the assistant pastor in a fundamentalist, Jesus-oriented church, who was teaching the small children's class before the regular church service. He decided to liven things up a bit by asking a riddle, so he said, "What has four legs, a bushy tail, climbs trees, and stores nuts for the winter?" The class considered, and then a small girl raised her hand. When called upon, she replied, "I know the answer is supposed to be Jesus, but it sure sounds like a squirrel to me."

report cards

Report cards can be a source of **conflicts,** but also a way of increasing understanding. The most important thing is to consider a report card and its **grades** as information about your performance (and possibly behavior) at school. When you read your report card, read it to see what you can learn from it. When you share it with your parents—and you always should, even if they don't ask to see it—encourage them to read it in the same way. It's fine, of course, to be praised for a good report, but it's hardly ever useful to be punished for a bad one. Rather, discuss with your parents what you intend to do to improve your work, if it should be better, and see if they have any advice.

As for teachers, if your report card is helpful and gives useful information, they'll probably appreciate being thanked, because conscientious teachers spend a lot of time doing reports. If there are grades or comments on the card that you don't fully understand, ask for an explanation. **Protesting** doesn't work. Never start **arguments** about a grade or comment. Instead, ask for the evidence and especially ask how you can improve your performance. If you think a grade is **unfair,** gently give your evidence but remember that the decision is the teacher's. Even if it doesn't get your grade changed for this time, it will show that you care and may help for next time.

One other point: Sometimes a report card provides a good basis for a **parent-teacher conference,** at which you too might be present, since you're the one who's going to have to deal with the results.

reputation

A person's reputation means how that person's character is seen or thought of by other people. Your reputation is based on how you have behaved in the past, what you have done and said—or what people *think* you have done and said. Obviously, it helps to get along with people if you have a good reputation, especially when it concerns **honesty, study habits,** behavior at social occasions like **parties,** and, sometimes, sexual behavior. (*See* **sex.**)

If you find that somehow you've gotten a bad reputation and you think you don't deserve it, put the question to a good friend or a trusted teacher. "I seem to have a reputation for [whatever it is]. I don't understand why. Can you help me understand? What should I do differently?" The answers to such questions, especially if you listen and don't jump in too quickly to defend yourself by saying "Yes, but . . . " or "That's not true!", can be a real help to you. *After* you have heard the answers, if there's some explaining to do, do it as factually as you can and help set the record straight.

If for some reason you get a bad reputation (say you cheated on tests a couple of times, or copied someone's work, or "borrowed" money from your parent's purse or wallet), you have to expect to be suspected for bad behavior the next time something like that happens, even if it wasn't you who did it. To get over a bad reputation, first state definitely to anyone important to you your determination never to act in that bad way again. *Admit* your mistake and *resolve* not to repeat it, and then *stick* to your determination and resolve. If *you* know you've changed your ways, that's the most important thing. In time, others will know—but it can take time.

Of course it's important, as far as the reputations of others are concerned, not to gossip or repeat rumors. Especially don't gossip about your parents or your teachers. (You don't want to get a reputation as a gossip.) Also, when you start with new teachers at the beginning of the school year, be careful not to judge those teachers on the basis of their reputation from last year. Collect your facts and experiences and make your own judgments—slowly.

Another very practical aspect of reputation concerns **jobs** you may hold, for the summer or part-time during the year. If you've done a good job, ask your employer for a written recommendation at the end of your job and keep these recommendations in a safe place. They can be your written reputation as a jobholder and help you when you want another job. Also, such careful behavior is likely to please your parents and impress your teachers.

responsibility

It's much easier to live with people who act responsibly than with those who don't. What is a responsible act? It is *responsibility* 108

an act that has good consequences, good results, for you and for all others affected by it, both for now and in the future. For example, doing your **chores** well, telling the truth, encouraging a discouraged person by honest **praise,** getting homework in on time and well done—these are responsible acts. Responsible, considerate actions please parents and teachers.

Some irresponsible acts would be: a child playing with matches in the living room (it may be fun, but it's likely to have bad consequences); a teenager having sexual intercourse so as to produce pregnancy or become pregnant (it may give pleasure at the moment, but in the future it will have damaging results); crashing **parties** (it may be fun while you do it, and people may even enjoy seeing you, but it leads to others doing the same thing, it puts the party at risk, and it gives you a bad **reputation**).

If you want to become more independent in your life, as most teenagers quite rightly do, you earn that right by acting responsibly. Obviously, you're unlikely to be perfectly responsible all the time. We all make **mistakes.** The thing to do is acknowledge them and learn from them, so that you're more responsible next time. (You can't expect your parents and teachers always to be responsible either. Even they make mistakes, and you will be kind—even responsible—if you point them out only tactfully and kindly.)

To be responsible requires two kinds of imagination. First, you have to be able to imagine yourself into the situation of those affected by your acts so you will know if the effects are good for them. And second, you have to project yourself into the future in order to know what the later consequences may be. You act now while considering the future.

A couple of other points: You are not responsible for your **feelings,** only for your actions. And you can't be responsible for all that your parents do—or, even less, all that your teachers do—even though you may *feel* responsible. You're a part of the family and the class, yes, but don't allow yourself to be too much burdened by them.

rewards

Two ways of affecting people's behavior are to reward them for good behavior and to punish them for bad behavior. In your life you have probably experienced a good deal of both, but there's no doubt that people do better, live together better, and enjoy life more if they get more rewards than **punishment**. So, in general, if possible, reward and **praise** the good more than condemning and punishing the bad. And if you find that your parents or your teachers seem to be scolding and punishing you more than praising and rewarding you, try this:

Think carefully about, say, the past week and jot down what you were scolded for and rewarded for at home and at school. Study the lists and see whether there are ways you can change your behavior to improve the situation. Discuss your home list with your parents and see what they think. If you can find a good time, discuss the school list with a teacher. It's quite possible that both parents and teachers may be surprised to see what their reward/punishment ratio actually is. And you, in turn, may discover some ways in which you can meet your own needs and at the same time be more rewardable and less punishable.

A few other points: Be sure you and your parents don't think of rewards as a sort of bribe—"If you do this, I'll pay you so much, or do that for you." The best rewards are appreciation, praise, and a feeling of gratefulness.

It is rarely a good idea to accept an arrangement by which you are paid for doing homework well or getting certain **grades** in school. Good schoolwork should be its own reward. Nor should doing regular **chores** be rewarded by payment. Chores are a part of keeping the life at home going well. Special **jobs** are another matter. Quite often, they probably should be paid for.

rights

At home and at school, you have both rights and responsibilities. Life is always pleasanter for your parents and teachers if you are mature and unselfish enough to give

rules

more attention to carrying out your responsibilities than to asserting your rights.

However, rights must be respected, yours, your parents', and your teachers'. What are your rights? You and your parents might find it fun and useful to make up a list. For starters, here's mine: You have a right to food, shelter, and clothing; to sleep; to respect from others; not to be hit or abused; to your **feelings,** including the right to be angry (but not always the right to express your feelings, which might damage others); to privacy; to an education; to the information you need to make decisions; to speak and be listened to; to explain; to have explanations of things you don't understand; to protest—or at least to question (but *not* to run things; you need limits and **rules**—in fact, you have a right to limits); to experiment and make some **mistakes**; to have some fun and **free time** to goof off now and then.

If you think your rights are not being respected, either at home or at school, don't be too quick to protest. But after considering the matter, if you think it's a serious problem, do bring it up and discuss it. Otherwise you may become downtrodden and weak, and nobody should make that the price for living together.

room *see* **your room/locker/desk**

rules

A fifth-grader once complained about school, "This is an awfully ruly classroom," and an older teacher with very well-established, unchangeable habits was described by a teenager as suffering from "hardening of the categories." Both these comments suggest that rules are a bother, a limitation of freedom, and a bad thing. Well, of course, sometimes they are, and when they are they should be discussed and changed.

However, if you think about it you'll realize that rules are a great help in enabling people to live together pleasantly and get on with what they want to accomplish. The rules may not have to be written down; they may just be accepted understandings or agreements. That's the way it is in most families. In schools, though, since so many more people are involved and order and good discipline are important, written rules are necessary. Rules that we all follow are helpful because they mean we can count on each other to behave in certain ways, to do certain things and not to do other things. If we had to figure everything out all over again every time we considered how to behave, it would be a terrible waste of time. Better to have some things settled so that we can use our energies and minds for more important tasks and purposes.

In a sense, rules give us an excuse *not* to think. This is good up to a point. However, if everything were covered by a rule, we'd never think at all but just go around feeling oppressed. Rules must be tested by whether or not they help the family or the school (or the whole nation, which has rules called laws, and regulations to carry them out) accomplish what needs to be done. If the rules seem to be more harmful than useful, they should be changed. The best policy for all of us is: obey the rules while they exist, but work together to change them if they are not useful and helpful.

Some commonsense rules for families are: do what you agree to do; tell the truth; respect people's property; respect people's ideas; respect people's feelings; respect people's bodies; do your chores; be on time—or explain why you can't be; when you've finished with something, put it away; don't invade other people's privacy; finish what you start, and if you can't, get help. You'll be able to think of others.

As for school, ask to see whatever rules are written down and agreed to by the staff. Also, if the teachers don't tell you, ask what the rules are for each classroom. (A really good teacher might reply, "Well, what do you think they should be?" and get the class to consider the matter.) Here are some rules that usually work well for almost any middle school or high school:

rules

1. Attend all classes and required activities and arrive on time.
2. Dress appropriately for the occasion and wear shoes.
3. Do not smoke, drink, or use drugs for nonmedical purposes.
4. Eat only in the lunchroom unless given permission to take lunch to a class or planned meeting.
5. Do not talk in places reserved for quiet study.
6. Do not run indoors.
7. Do not make loud noises indoors.
8. Do not take, borrow, or interfere with other people's belongings or school property.
9. Tell the truth.
10. Do not plagiarize (copy other people's work).
11. Do not use offensive language.
12. Do not litter.
13. Do not leave the school grounds without proper permission.

Some suggestions about rules: If you think someone is going against a rule at home or at school, don't say "This is the rule; obey it!" Instead, say something like "What's the rule about food from the fridge?" or "What's the rule about looking in other people's desks?" Saying it that way gets the other person thinking and not feeling scolded.

Instead of merely **protesting** about rules you don't like, find times to express your gratefulness for the rules that work: "I'm sure glad we have a rule about knocking on a closed door of a room rather than barging in."

Making Up Rules

Assume that your family or your school or your classroom has no rules at all. Make up a set of rules you think would work well. Put a question mark beside those you're not sure about. Then discuss your list with the family or classmates and teacher. See if you can agree on a set of rules that would really work and be helpful. If you think it would be a good idea, have somebody write up the rules on a large sheet of paper and post it, putting a date and maybe a title on it.

running away

Almost every teenager or young child has at some time felt like running away from home, just to get away from it all. It's a natural feeling, to want to escape from problems. Of course, there are smaller ways of escaping—we can run away into a good book or TV program, to a friend's house, or just to our room for a couple of hours. That kind of running away or escape is healthy—even necessary from time to time. But actually to run away from home, to leave with the intention of not coming back and to do it secretly, is very dangerous. It's also illegal for minors. You can be arrested for running away, just as you can for playing hookey from school, for being a truant.

If you ever seriously consider running away from home, my advice, most urgently given, is *don't!* Hold on. Somehow work out your problems. Get help. It's a tough, cold world out there, and runaway teenagers are very likely to be picked up by people who act like friends, who "save" them from troubles, and then get them into using drugs and selling drugs or into sex and prostitution, from which it is extremely difficult to get disentangled.

If, because of sexual, physical, or psychological abuse at home, or because you've gotten into serious trouble with drugs or theft and are afraid you'll get busted, you feel you just can't stand being at home and have to leave, at least wait long enough to talk with someone about it. Get up your courage and tell your parents, one or both, what you feel like doing, and make it clear that it's urgent. If you absolutely can't talk to your parents, try a teacher or the parents of a friend, asking them to keep secret what you tell them, at least until you can get things figured out.

If none of that works, maybe you have to leave. At least tell your parents what you're doing and why. Tell them that you're going to stay with a friend or relative. You can ask them not to get in touch with you until you've had a chance to get yourself together. You can promise to be in touch with them soon. You can ask them not to tell the police. Then, when you've gone, do get messages to them saying that you're all right, or ask someone else they know to get that message to them.

A really critical, urgent action like this—not exactly running away secretly and, as far as parents know, forever—will make your parents realize that changes have to be made. It may force some deep thinking and some deep communication. However, to run away, or even go away without permission and arrangements agreed upon in advance, is almost certainly bad business. It's much better to face the problems together and figure out what has to be changed to make life together possible.

Two suggestions: Getting away from your family for a period of relief and change, a sort of vacation, may be an excellent thing to do. Talk about it and see if you can't agree on whom you might go to—perhaps a relative or a good friend's house—for a change you feel you must have. If you are really going to run away, or if you have run away, look in the white pages of your telephone book under Runaway or call the National Runaway Switchboard (1-800-621-4000) and talk with them. Your call will be confidential. You'll not be asked your name unless you want to give it. But help will be offered if you want to accept it. They will also relay messages to your parents if you ask them to, and without revealing where you are.

secrets

If parents and teachers and teenagers keep too many things secret from one another, it makes it harder to live together. "Yes, but—" you say, and you're right. Total **openness** would be a disaster!

So we all have secrets. Some we keep entirely to ourselves. Some we tell only to our best friends, or perhaps to a parent or a brother or sister, or a grandparent who listens well and tells nothing. We want people to respect our secrets, and we must respect theirs.

However, my first sentence is right too—too much

secrecy makes living together difficult. The more open we can be with each other in our families, the better—provided, of course, that family members don't tell people the private things and feelings that are a part of the life of all families. (If you feel that family secrets are being spread about, say so and tell how it makes you feel.)

What about school? Are there things about school that should be kept secret? There's the confidential information you share with a teacher or counselor. Also, there may be times when in a class discussion someone uses his or her own family life as an example of some sort of human behavior (cruelty, selfishness, sharing feelings, fighting, for example). It's only respectful not to spread this information outside the class. Also, it's much better to tell about such things indirectly: "Supposing a father really beats on his kids . . . " or "I know there are families where nobody dares admit any mistake or bad behavior because . . . " This is better than saying, "In my family . . . " or "In Sally's family . . . " It enables a class to talk about basic problems of human behavior without betraying secrets.

One other matter. Suppose a friend asks, "May I tell you something? Will you promise not to tell a soul?" What should you do? The natural first reaction is, "Of course. Tell me. I won't tell anybody." But the trouble with this is that perhaps the secret thing that you are being told really shouldn't be kept secret, as, for example, that some kids are planning to damage some property or that so-and-so is stealing money from the class treasury. For the benefit of all, these sorts of information should not be kept secret. Therefore, do not make **promises** not to tell. Instead, you can say, "I promise I won't tell unless I really think it would be bad not to. And I will promise not to tell anyone without telling you first that I'm going to, and who I'm going to tell, and maybe you'll tell with me." This is usually OK with the person who wants to share a secret, and rarely do you have to reveal the secret to anyone else.

There's one other situation where you may feel that confidential information about you is being shared in a way you don't like, and that is in **parent-teacher conferences.** You should try to be present at such conferences, to hear what's said and to say what you feel needs saying.

selfishness

To be totally selfish is to be concerned only about yourself, to work only for your own pleasure and comfort, and not to consider the well-being of other people. It's almost impossible to live with a totally selfish person, and such people need help. However, all of us are—and should be—a little bit selfish. That is, we need to see to it that our own needs are met. And if we fling ourselves totally into serving others, we may become pretty difficult to live with.

Also, it's hard on people to require them to try to figure out what we need because we're so "unselfish" we won't tell them. What we must try to do, of course, is to be aware of what those we live with want and need, whether at home or at school, and to help provide it if we can—that's really unselfish. But also we must make our own needs known so that others can have the pleasure and satisfaction of helping us provide for those needs. There's pleasure in helping; there's pleasure in being helped, especially if we express appreciation.

What if someone, a teacher or a parent, tells you you're acting selfishly? It may come as a shock. It's natural to resent it. But try to listen, to learn what it is that seems selfish, and to change your ways. You may not realize that you're demanding too much of a teacher's time, for example, or that your tapes or telephone conversations are annoying your parents. It's "selfish" to be unaware, but if you're told about it, you can change your ways. And if you can change your ways with a smile, and with a comment like "I'm really sorry; I never realized" or even "If I do something like that again, please tell me," it makes it all the better.

On the other hand, if you live with others who seem selfish and unaware of the effects on others of their actions, what do you do? Saying "Hey, you're really selfish when you do that" may work, but probably it will just arouse resentment. It's better to choose your time carefully and start with "May I tell you something?" Then, if the answer is something like "Sure, go ahead," you can explain in a low-key, objective way what the problem is: "When you use the bathroom just when I have to catch the school bus . . . " or "When you give us only a couple of minutes to copy down our homework assignment . . . " or "It really would be great if we could work out a way to use our homeroom after lunch instead of being locked out." You may find that your parents or your teachers were unaware of the effects of their actions and just needed to know—a very curable selfishness.

Unselfish Acts

A good device to use at home now and then is to have a sort of family meeting when you can go around the circle and each person tell an *un*selfish thing that somebody else in the family did in the past week ("Mom brought my lost homework to school for me after I couldn't find it"; "George just got up and washed the dishes because I was so exhausted I fell asleep on the sofa"; "Last Tuesday, Dad went out and bought everybody an ice-cream cone and delivered them to us wherever we were because we all seemed so depressed"; your family meeting can lengthen the list). The same sort of meeting can work at school too, as can an assignment to write a paper titled "Two Unselfish Acts I Remember and What the Results Were." Maybe this sounds corny, but it works when the papers are read aloud, either in small groups or to the whole class.

Treat Yourself

Another device that works is just to admit that you need a good, solid, pure bit of pleasure, a treat—to please yourself. You stop working, you go to the fridge or the TV or the corner store or your room, and you spend half an hour or a couple of dollars on whatever you want that doesn't hurt anybody else. Then you can go back to being unselfish again.

"Why I Would Like . . . "
One way to get outside yourself for a little while and at the same time examine yourself is to have members of the family write a few paragraphs on either of these two subjects: "Why I would like to have myself as a child" or, for your parents, "Why I would like to have myself as a parent." Taking the opposite tack can be even more fun: "Why *I wouldn't* like to have myself . . . " Be sure people write knowing that they will be sharing, discussing, and even arguing (in the highest sense of the word!) about the papers.

Another possibility is to do the same thing speaking as student and teacher.

sense of humor   *see* humor

sex
Teenagers, parents, teachers—all of us—are interested in the subject of sex, and yet very often we find it difficult to talk about with each other. Somehow, you're not supposed to talk frankly and openly about human sexuality, even though the media—especially records and tapes, magazines, TV—"talk" to us about it quite noisily much of the time. So our society has been called "sex-noisy *and* sex-silent." Anything you can do to make yourself and others sex-informed and sex-thoughtful, instead of "silent" or "noisy," will help you deal with your own sexuality in more responsible ways. It will also help you live in better understanding with your parents and at least some of your teachers. (For teachers of many subjects, human sexuality is not relevant.)

As a start, it's a good idea to know the right answers to six often misunderstood questions about human sexuality.

1. Is sex the same as genitals (vagina, clitoris, penis, testicles, etc.)? No. Years ago a salesman showed me a plastic model of the human body, including the circulatory

system, the digestive system, and the nervous system—but between the navel and the knee the whole thing was blank. "What about the reproductive system?" I asked. "Well," he replied, "you know how sensitive people are about that." I pressed him a bit, and finally he produced a small cardboard carton containing two compartments, one with the female system, one with the male. The price on the box was $14.95. He proudly showed me how you could unplug the blank area and put in either male genitals or female genitals. I thought to myself, "What a false lesson! The only difference between men and women is a $14.95 set of genitals." We need to unlearn this idea. Sexuality is much more complicated than that.

2. Is sex bad? No. Our sexuality is neither bad nor good. It *exists*. What is bad or good is how we use it.

3. Is sex the best thing and the greatest pleasure there is? Not necessarily. For some people, perhaps it is. For others, it's not very important. There are also other great pleasures: ideas, humor, beauty, helping others, faith in God, exercise, family love. Sex for most people is *one* of life's great pleasures.

4. Do you have to be sexually active to stay alive, or at least to stay healthy? No. There are millions of people who are not sexually active who have wonderful, healthy, fulfilled lives.

5. Do you prove yourself by how much sex you have, by how often you have intercourse or with how many people? Again, this is just not true. Rabbits are often said to be the champion animal copulators. If you try to prove yourself by the quantity of your sexual activity, all you prove is that you are a better rabbit.

6. Is sex natural? No, it is not. Yes, of course, it *is* a part of our nature, but much of our sexual behavior is cultural: we learn it. Cows and bulls, rams and ewes, cocks and hens have sex the same way all over the world, but not people. With us it depends on the culture we live in.

What you need to learn are the facts about human reproduction; the facts about heredity; the facts about human sexual feelings; and the pros and cons on some of the major issues about sex and reproduction—such as abortion, contraception (birth control), masturbation, necking and petting, dating and going steady, premarital intercourse, homosexuality, **sex roles** (the differences in the ways men and women behave), sexually transmitted diseases (STD, or VD), the relationship between sex and **love**, and so forth—and you need opportunities to discuss all these matters both in the family and among your peers, coeducationally, so that you can think things through before you are faced with having to make heavy decisions about sex.

Obviously, this book is not the place to give all this information or to set forth all these issues. But a book of facts is a useful means for informing yourself and for opening up the subject with your parents. One book I can recommend (because I wrote it) is *Love and Sex in Plain Language*. It can be read by both you and your parents.

Here are some suggestions about human sexuality, your own education, and your parents. If you have questions about sex, ask them—not suddenly, but at a good time. You'll probably find that your parents are just waiting for you to bring them up. Remember that your parents, quite rightly, are much concerned about your sexual life, both now and in the future. They want the best for you and are scared that you'll get into trouble—especially that you may go "too far" or get pregnant or make somebody pregnant. When your parents answer your questions, they may tell you things you already know, or think you know. Don't say, in words or by your expression, "Gee, I'm not an infant. I know all that stuff." Listen, learn, and ask more questions. Maybe you don't know as much as you think you do.

Don't ask your parents personal questions about their own sexual lives. That's private. Be careful about the **words** and **language** you use in discussing sexuality. If you know them, use the "correct" words: penis, vagina, intercourse. Slang words for sexual matters are shocking to many people and can make **communication** more difficult.

Here are some suggestions about your teachers and

sex. Again, use correct words. If your school doesn't have a sex education course, say that you wish it would start one and explain why. If you can, get your parents to back you up. Keep in mind that teachers and school administrators are quite concerned that there may be opposition in the community if they start a sex education program that goes beyond the simple facts of reproduction and, maybe, venereal disease. These opponents are very convinced, emotional, and often well organized. They can have a big influence, and they are usually strong and sincere. But all surveys have shown that 75 to 80 percent of families favor sex education in the schools, so it's not fair for a minority to keep it out (though they do have the right to ask that their own children not participate). And remember that what schools should teach in sex education is not *how to* but *what is.* They teach *about* sex, not "sex in the classroom."

In relating to your parents and teachers on matters of sex education, you can learn more and with fewer objections if you agree that whatever education there is at home or at school be based on so-called "moral" values. Here are eight values I first listed in my book *Love and Sex in Plain Language,* stated in a way I think almost everyone, religious or not, can agree with.

1. The first value is the *infinite worth of each individual person.* This includes yourself and others. Don't forget that self-respect is the beginning of respect for others.

2. The second value is *consideration.* You consider and care both for your own needs, feelings, worth, and welfare and also for those of others. To be truly considerate of others, you must have enough thoughtfulness and imagination to put yourself in their shoes, to try to understand their situation and their ways of thinking and feeling. (*See* **responsibility.**)

3. The third value is *communication.* It is good to be able to talk things over with other people. How else can you know their needs, thoughts, and feelings, and how else can they consider yours? It is good for people to be

able to talk with each other about their sexual feelings, desires, and fears.

4. The fourth value is the *family*. The family is one of the main bases of a healthy society, and for most people the best way to grow up is as part of a healthy, loving, sharing family. You should consider your sexual actions on the basis of whether they will strengthen and enrich your family, the families of others, and any family you may help to create.

5. The fifth value is *responsibility*. If you are a responsible person, before you act you think about what the results of your action will be. You consider the results of these actions not only for yourself but also for others, and not just for today but for the future as well.

6. The sixth value is *pleasure and good feelings*. We all know, and have known since we were infants, that our bodies can give us good feelings. For many people—though not all—feelings of bodily pleasure, called sensual feelings, are an important part of a good life, right through old age.

7. The seventh value is *control*. Sex is a power. Like any other power, it can be used for good or for bad. You learn to control your sexual power so that you use it for good—the good of yourself and of others.

8. The eighth value is *information*. Correct information—the facts—is better than ignorance or rumor. Sound information makes it possible for you to act responsibly. Ignorance may get you into trouble.

sex roles

One of the difficulties some boys and girls have at home and at school is that they don't behave the way "a nice girl" or "a real boy" is supposed to behave. They don't act out their sex roles. A typical boy or man's role is to be vigorous, aggressive, and decisive; a typical girl or woman's role is to be sweet, gentle, with a desire to please. In order to live harmoniously with parents and teachers, you need to keep in mind what kinds of behavior they may expect of you as a boy or girl so that you don't annoy or shock them too much. This doesn't mean that you should spinelessly accept the role expected of you, only that you be aware of what people may be expecting and allow for it in your daily life, and also that you respect their feelings even if you do not share them. (And, of course, maybe you *do* share them.) In many cases, as you probably are aware, older people tend to believe in "proper" sex roles more than younger ones do.

Actually, there are some strong influences both in our society and in our bodies and body chemistry that cause males and females to tend to speak or act "in a different voice," to use the phrase of Harvard psychologist Carol Gilligan. For example: obviously it's only women who become pregnant, give birth to babies, and, usually, spend most time taking care of them when they are small. Also, men's bodies produce more of a hormone called testosterone, which, in addition to causing secondary sex characteristics like beards and the generally (not always) larger, more muscular bodies of men, also helps cause vigorous behavior. (Women's bodies also produce testosterone, but in smaller quantities.) Further, from the very moment they are born, girl babies and boy babies tend to be handled a bit differently by their parents and nurses and so forth: boys a bit more vigorously, girls a bit more delicately.

In her book *In a Different Voice,* Carol Gilligan carefully makes the point that the typical "masculine voice" is neither better nor worse, stronger or weaker, than the typical "feminine voice." What she says is that they are different and that the world needs both. (She also says that about a third of men act and think more like typical women, and about a third of women act more like typical men—which is an observed fact, not a criticism of either.) Gilligan says that men tend to be concerned more with the "ethics of justice" (making rules, doing things the right and *just* way regardless of the effects), while women tend to be concerned with the "ethics of caring" (rules are less important than *caring* about the effects of our actions on other people, the effects of actions on the context surrounding them). Men tend to be more concerned about reaching their **goals,** about achieving success no matter who gets bumped, whereas women tend to be more concerned about what happens to others as they work toward their goals.

Fortunately, these days men and women are generally much freer to be what they want to be and behave as they feel they should. They are much less limited by sex roles imposed by society. What I am suggesting is that you pay attention to the ethics of caring and try to keep aware of the effects of your actions on others, especially your parents and teachers. Be true to yourself, but respect the feelings and expectations of others.

If a parent or teacher says to you something like "That's no way for a boy [or a girl] to act," listen, express interest, and ask what the person means. "Really? How do you think a girl [or boy] should act?" "Why do you think so?" This can get a good discussion going.

His-and-Her Adjectives

As a sort of game or discussion stimulator, write down a list of adjectives and then have the players check whether they are more descriptive of the behavior of boys or girls (men or women). Some adjectives you might use are: vigorous, weak, tender, emotional, sweet, caring, rude, noisy, purposeful, gentle, rough, silly, sexy, courageous, intelligent, honest, reliable, gossipy, cheerful, considerate. These are twenty; think of some more. Boxes you might check would be: Are this way ☐ always; ☐ usually; ☐ some of the time; ☐ hardly ever; ☐ never, with a separate set of check spaces for boys and for girls. One last check could be: Which are more likely to be this way? ☐ boys; ☐ girls; ☐ about the same; ☐ don't know. Comparing answers and giving examples to support what you checked can help make you more aware of the reactions of others.

smoking

If you are a teenager and don't smoke, don't start! It's usually a bad way to live with people, whether they be other teenagers, teachers, or parents. A few years ago, it was considered a sign of being grown up and cool to light up and take a drag. But today, with everything doctors and scientists know about the health dangers of smoking, it's foolishness to start or to continue. It *doesn't* make you mature, sexy, or virile, no matter what the cigarette ads may suggest.

However, there's no doubt that smoking is still very much a part of our culture. About one third of adults smoke regularly, although the percentage is going down. Also, there's no doubt that the nicotine in cigarettes is a drug. That is, it affects our bodies as drugs do, and it is addictive, both physically and psychologically. Only about a third of habitual smokers who try to get off smoking succeed. As the saying goes, "Sure, it's easy to give up smoking. I've done it dozens of times." Therefore, to live well with parents who are smokers, you have to respect the likelihood that smoking gives them pleasure and that giving up smoking will be painful. Constant nagging by you would not be a good idea.

On the other hand, you'll do your parents (and your teachers) a favor if you can find ways to convince them to stop smoking. Certainly you have a right to object absolutely and at once if a teacher smokes in class or in the halls. You have a right, also, to refuse to stay in the room with a parent who smokes. After all, the living room, the dining room, and the kitchen are family "public areas." If possible, *you* stay; ask your *parents* to go somewhere else—and explain why! One of the reasons for doing this is that "passive smoking," which is the involuntary inhaling of the smoky air in a room where someone else is smoking, can be bad for your health. Another reason is that, presumably, you prefer healthy parents to sick ones, ones who may suffer from serious illnesses and die earlier than they would if they didn't smoke. However, be sure that your parents or your teachers know that it's the smoking that's terrible, not they as people.

Some facts about smoking are that most habitual smokers start young and then can't stop. Also, pregnant mothers who smoke have a higher rate of miscarriages than nonsmokers and are more likely to have sickly, defective, or retarded babies. Also, as doctors John E. Schowalter and Walter R. Anyan write in *The Family Book of Adolescence,* "Life is shortened by fourteen minutes for every cigarette smoked and inhaled. Cancer of the lung favors smokers eleven to one, and under the age of sixty-five, smokers are two or three times as likely to die of heart disease as nonsmokers."

standards

People's standards are the rules and measures by which they decide how they are going to behave and what they are going to do. Standards apply in many areas of life. You sometimes hear people say something like "Well, his standards are too high for me" or "She's just got no standards at all when it comes to schoolwork" or "Boy, standards of **honesty** [or **language, appearance, music, manners,** or whatever] just aren't what they used to be!"

As a part of our own self-respect, we all establish standards for ourselves, and both our parents and teachers and our peers have a lot of influence on what those standards are. Within a school, it's usually a useful challenge to have standards we must try to meet, standards of behavior and standards of academic performance—**grades.** It's also very important to know what standards teachers expect in their classrooms, in the work they assign, and so forth. "She has really high standards" can be a great compliment to a teacher unless the standards are so high that most students can't meet them. In that case, discussion and exchange of ideas may work well. **Rebellion** won't.

Compared to those at school, standards at home are usually far less definite. Also they are learned gradually as the years go by. Teenagers who live with parents who have good standards are fortunate, even though it is a natural and good part of growing up to challenge the standards. Challenges and the discussion of standards lead to maturity and to learning to live well on your own.

Here are some suggestions: At school, find out what the standards are and try to live up to them. Be considerate of your parents' standards even if you disagree with some of them. Develop standards of your own—of course you will, whether I tell you to or not—and be ready to explain them. It's good for teenagers to have strong standards, but they should not be too rigid. Try not to *impose* your standards on others, but rather, if you believe in them strongly, explain and promote them by example. Always be ready to listen to suggestions about how they might be different. *See also* **ideals; rules; values; generation gap.**

stealing *see* **honesty; reputation**

stepparents *see* **divorce**

study habits

Unfortunately, some parents and teachers are convinced that there is only one proper, efficient way to study and learn subject matter in school. In fact, different people learn in different ways, and no simple prescription works for everyone. The most important thing for you is to develop the way that works best for you. If it clearly does work well, your parents and teachers will be satisfied, even if it doesn't exactly fit their ideas. But if it doesn't fit, take the trouble to explain what your system is and how it works for you.

On the other hand, quite a few teenagers seem to fall apart in their efforts to manage their time and learning, and yet they don't quite have the courage to admit it. They flop around, don't do well in school, and this often worries their parents and teachers, makes them angry, and leads to a lot of friction. If you are in that state, ask whether the school *study habits*

or a teacher can provide some help in getting your methods of study and learning into good working order.

Here are some suggestions for study habits (you might want to share and discuss them with your parents or teachers): Write down your assignments in a special notebook, with date due. Plan a regular schedule for homework—independent study—at home. Have a quiet place to work equipped with the necessities: pencils, pen, paper, dictionary, calendar, good light. Be certain you understand the purpose of an assignment before you do it. If you can't figure it out, ask (tactfully).

Skim over any reading assignment *rapidly* before reading it carefully—glance at the headings, titles, and paragraph beginings, just to get an idea of what's involved. (See **reading**.) Use any study aids in the book—italicized words, lists, charts, maps, questions at the end. Pause after each section of the book and see if you can recall what it said. (Don't do this with stories or novels.) If you own the book, mark it as you read to help recall the main ideas. Look up new words. When you've finished the material, think back and recall, even jot down, the main ideas. Note down anything that isn't clear and raise questions in class. Also see if you are able to answer end-of-chapter questions.

Note and deal with all corrections and suggestions made to you in class and on your papers. If you have a long-term assignment, plan your time.

Learn to make a rough outline for organizing your ideas or reviewing for **tests**. When reviewing for tests, use your mark-ups, study aids in the books, and notes on teachers' comments in class. Spend your time on the parts you don't know. Find a way to make yourself be interested in the work. Beware of "I'm bored!".

Not all these suggestions may work well for you. Some people have "odd" study habits that fit their own needs. For example:

You may be a *slow shifter*. You get deeply into a subject and have a hard time shifting to another. Some of the greatest minds in the world work this way. If that's your way, recognize it and explain it to parents and teachers.

You may be a *moody worker.* Some times of the day, or on some days, you are a whiz; at other times you are not much good. Recognize this and benefit from your good times—but don't use "I'm not in the mood" as an excuse for failure. You've got to learn to manage your moods.

You may be a *physical learner.* You need to get up and pace about, work for a spurt and then lie down. (You may even write and read better lying down than sitting at a desk or table.) OK, but let your parents know this. Also, at school, in most situations you've just got to fit in with the system—and the desk.

You may be a *talking learner,* doing best if you can share and discuss with parents, siblings, classmates, teachers, and friends the materials you are studying. Again, OK, if it doesn't bother others.

You may be a *slow learner.* That doesn't mean your intelligence is low but that you learn materials very thoroughly and slowly, as you think about them and argue (in your mind) with what you're reading. Again, OK if you can meet essential deadlines.

You may work best as a *last-minute artist.* You thrive on pressure; for a two-week project, you get your materials only a couple of days ahead, read all night, and write frantically till the moment the work is due—and it turns out to be excellent. If you're this way and it works well, *explain* to your teachers and parents so they won't think you're just a goof-off.

On the other hand, you may be a *buckler under pressure.* You tend to collapse if you're pressed and hurried. Allow for this and try to work out a way to get your major assignments well in advance. Let your parents know that you need time.

Touch-typing—typing correctly and rapidly without having to look at the keyboard—is a tremendous advantage in doing written projects for school and college and, later, on the job. Touch-typing also makes it much easier to use word processors and computers. Learn it while you are young and can do it easily. Teachers are always delighted to receive a clearly typed, double-spaced paper.

suicide

There's no question that for many teenagers life's problems are really tough to take. Many feel all messed up inside their heads: they feel that they are no good at anything, a real burden on the people who have to live with them; that nobody really loves or understands them or can possibly understand how miserable they are. Common thoughts are, "If I die, *then* they'll realize how much they miss me" or "It'd just be simpler if I was dead—after all, I never asked to be born" or "I'd really be doing everybody a favor if I just stopped living."

Well, obviously, committing suicide is a very poor way of living with teachers and parents. And far from being unselfish, it is a supremely selfish act. It results in terrible anguish for those left behind, especially parents, who will ask themselves for the rest of their lives, "What could we have done to prevent it?" Or they will feel, "It was our fault." Also, suicide is the ultimate form of running away. You can't come back; you'll never know how things might have been made better.

Here are some facts about suicide: It is the second leading cause of death among people aged 10 to 24. (The leading cause is accidents.) In surveys of teenagers, 85 percent say they have thought about suicide, and 50 percent have seriously considered it. Probably most suicides are really a cry for help, not a genuine desire to die. This explains why so many teenagers (and adults, too) make a halfhearted attempt at suicide, in a way that won't really kill them—just dramatically announce their suffering and stress and say to people, "Now, listen to my troubles!" Three main reasons for teenage suicide, or attempts at suicide, are not feeling valued and appreciated; feeling they are a burden on those around them and on themselves; and setting such high expectations for themselves that they can't possibly meet them.

So what to do to avoid this terrible and tragic breakdown in relationships? Do talk about it—with somebody. If the response (say, from your parents) is "Oh, you don't really feel that way" or "Things aren't that bad" or "Come on! That's nonsense. Pull yourself together," find someone else to talk to—a teacher, a friend, a counselor, the family doctor. If talking about it doesn't seem to get through, try writing down your feelings and what you think causes them. Be specific if you can. And write down what you think needs to be changed to make your feelings of wanting to die go away. Keep what you've written and read it over. Then find somebody to show it to. It may well help you to start talking deeply with a parent or teacher about your troubles and feelings. A written statement, even just rough notes, can make people pay attention.

If your suicidal feelings are deep and frequent, it's obvious that you need **help**, even though you probably don't want to admit it. Expert, caring, loving help *is* available. A psychiatrist often can provide what you need, or a special psychiatric counselor. Do talk with your parents about this. Insist on your need. If you somehow can't make yourself talk with them, call a local *suicide hotline*, listed under Suicide Prevention in your telephone book. Counselors will talk, listen, keep confidences, and tell you how to get help.

swearing   *see* cursing

talking things over

In almost every case, it's better to talk over pleasures and problems and **conflicts** than to stay silent about them. Talking is **communication**—a way of sharing **feelings, ideals, goals**—and people who share by talking live together better than people who don't. You may feel some things are too private to share. OK, it's your life. And there are times when it's better to postpone talking it over, as when the other person is very busy or very angry and *talking things over* 132

upset. But even then it's good to say, "Let's find a time to talk about [whatever it is]."

Talking something over can be done at some specifically arranged times (often best with teachers, whose lives are very scheduled) or just as part of the general conversation around the house (best with parents). It's useful to keep a sort of mental list of things you'd like to talk about so that you're ready when opportunities come—maybe while doing the dishes or gardening or driving together in the car. (*See also* arguments; listening; negotiating.)

We Need to Talk About . . .

One family has a WE NEED TO TALK ABOUT chalkboard in the kitchen, on which members of the family jot down items that are on their minds. It's amazing how well this device works.

Here are some kinds of questions you can ask parents, and they can ask you when you see each other, just to get the talk going: How was your day? What was the worst [best] part of your day? Did you get, hear, or read any new idea today? Did anything surprise you today? What are you most looking forward to in the next few days? What things are worrying you most today—or these days? Stimulating questions like these, or statements by you about these subjects, help to bring families together, and often they're fun to think and hear about.

Sitcom Sessions

A useful way to talk about yourself and your problems and pleasures, or those of your parents, without embarrassing people, is to do it *indirectly*. If you have all watched a TV program together, quite often you may find that characters in the program have some of the same problems and feelings that you have, or quite opposite ones from yours. As the family reacts together about the TV character, you may all come to understand each other somewhat better. You are "talking things over" once removed.

The same thing works at home, and especially at school, if you discuss the people and events in books the whole class has read.

Two other things: If you really don't feel like talking about something, that's quite natural. You can just say, "I don't feel like talking about it now. Maybe later, OK?" And if your parents, seeing that you are looking and acting miserable, ask, "What's the matter?" don't say, "Oh, nothing." If you possibly can, tell them. (The same could go for teachers.) And if your parents (or even a teacher) seem upset or unhappy, ask, with concern, "What's the matter? Can I help?" (Not "What's the matter *now*?!")

Topic Talking
Make up a set of index cards, each with a topic written on it—any interesting topics. Here are some possible ones: money, marriage, griping, enemies, habits, heaven, cheating, daydreams, alcohol, drinking, clothes, yelling, work, ugliness, religion, weapons, rewards, surprises, sleep, words, self-control, jungles. You'll be able to think of dozens more. Make from fifty to a hundred topic cards. Then sit around a table as in a game, shuffle the cards, and take turns picking one. Read the subject and say briefly whatever you want to say about it, serious or funny or both. When you're done, let each person add one or two sentences or, if they wish, just pass. (If a topic card gets the family into a good discussion, fine. That's what it's all about.) Nobody "wins" this game, or loses.

talebearing *see* honesty

teacher's pet
In elementary school most kids like to please their teachers and like to be approved of, even though if a teacher approves too much it may make other kids say, in a teasing way, "Teacher's pet—yah! yah!" But by the time people reach adolescence, this approval is usually not so good. You're probably becoming more interested in getting along

teacher's pet

with your peers (see **peer pressure**) than you are in pleasing your teachers. There are quite a few teenagers who try *not* to do well, or not to be conspicuously praised by teachers, because it's not the "in" thing. You are very fortunate if you go to a school where doing well academically and behaving well in school are OK with the peer group. If not—if doing well in your work and getting a lot of teacher praise for it is making life difficult for you with your friends—here are some things you might try.

Find a time to tell teachers that you want to do well and are glad to know that you are doing well, but be frank in explaining what sort of trouble too much public praise is causing you. Most teachers will understand and will respect you for your honesty. Be careful not to seem too quick and eager to please and to answer questions. Give others a chance, and encourage them.

Don't make the unwise choice of doing less than your best in order to keep friends. A good education is too important for that. Maybe, instead, you can persuade a few friends to get on the good-performance path with you. It's a great way to get along with teachers, whereas doing less than your best is a poor way.

Of course, there's an even worse problem than being a teacher's pet, and that is being a teacher's victim, the one who always seems to get blamed for things. If you're in that situation, set out to prove by your academic performance and general behavior that you are a good and accomplishing member of the class. Find a time to ask the teacher what the trouble is. If it turns out that for some reason, probably for past behavior, you've gotten a bad **reputation** and teachers don't know you've changed, again, find a chance to talk it over, admit any past wrongdoing (this can win you only respect), and explain that you think you've mended your ways and learned from your mistakes. You can even ask teachers to tell you, if possible privately, when you are not behaving as well or doing as well as you are trying to.

teasing

In almost all families where people enjoy one another and feel comfortable and free together, there's teasing. It's a part of human behavior. It's also a part of animal behavior. Watch dogs playing. They nip and snarl and shove and chase and bark in a lively way, almost like fighting, but if one dog goes too far, the other dog will suddenly snarl or growl in a different way or give a serious snap with its teeth, and that means it feels threatened. It's not in fun any more. Almost always the other dog will recognize the "cut it out!" signal and go off and lie down till things have cooled off.

It's good if teenagers and their parents recognize the "cut it out" signs that people make. Teasing is a good subject to talk about now and then in families. The main thing is to know when you're going too far. If you're hurting the other person, stop, no matter how much fun you thought you were having. If, on the other hand, you're feeling hurt, say so—maybe not with a grim snarl or a slap; just say, "That hurts." Then, if you can, smile.

In school, teachers quite often tease students they are fond of or who they think are secure and will enjoy it. Being teased in that way is a compliment. But if you really don't like it or are embarrassed by it, say so—probably after class. In the same way, always remembering to be basically respectful, you can help some teachers enjoy life more by some affectionate teasing. I remember visiting the tenth-grade class of an excellent history teacher. While we were waiting for class to begin, I asked a bright-looking kid, "What's the most important thing you've learned in this class so far this year?" The boy replied, after making sure that the teacher could hear, "We've learned two things. One: all history books are wrong. Two: only Mrs. Reifsnyder is perfect." Mrs. R. was delighted and laughed louder than anyone else. That's good teasing.

telephone

In many families, who gets to use the telephone, when, and how much is a source of friction. And yet it should be

telephone a fairly easy problem to solve by simply sitting down and agreeing to some **rules** or procedures. There's no doubt that quite often you may need to touch base with a friend, share a bit of news, or get help with a school problem; while your father may need to organize a committee meeting or talk to your grandmother; and at the same time your mother may be arranging something about her work or just relaxing with a friend by talking—and all of these can't happen at the same time.

Here are some suggestions. Try to plan your long telephone calls when no one else is at home or needs the phone, and tactfully suggest this to your parents too. Agree that, if possible, when others are in the house, you won't stay on the phone for longer than 10 or 15 minutes. Remember, there may be people out there in the great world who are trying to get through to your family, and a constant busy signal is very frustrating. Therefore, try to leave a few minutes between calls so that others can get through.

Tell your parents in advance (and siblings, too) if you know you're going to need an extra long time on the phone, and plan that sort of call in advance. The friend you are talking with probably has no way of knowing that other people need to use your phone, so don't hesitate to say, "We've got to quit in a couple of minutes. There's a lineup for the phone," or something else to clue in your friend. Agree on a signal if you or your parents urgently need the phone while someone is talking on it. Maybe a little card reading URGENT NEED! could be kept by the phone and turned over when needed.

Of course there are confidential, even secret things you may want to share with a friend on the phone. So you'll talk in a low voice. But if you whisper for a long time, and look around suspiciously as you do so, it's a pretty good way to make parents feel something really terrible is being shared. Therefore, if you can, after such a session, apologize a little and at least mention the subject you were talking about, if not the details, or say, "Boy, *that* was a gossip session! But don't worry. No crimes are being planned and the world isn't coming to an end."

Never, but never, try to sneak in a period of listening on an extension, even though you may have to pick up briefly to know whether or not the phone is in use.

Some teenagers arrange to have their own phone and a separate line in their rooms. This may be OK if the family can afford it. An even better way, if you feel you really need your own phone, is to earn the money to have it installed and pay for it yourself. But be sure to talk it over with your parents and get full approval first. Having your own phone requires you to develop good self-control, or you may allow the phone to rule your life and mess up your **chores** and **study habits.**

television *see* TV

tests

In some ways one could say that all of life is a test of one sort or another, although that could be a pretty grim way to look at it. ("Am I passing? Am I failing?" Oof!) Maybe it's better to say that life is a gift to be enjoyed, and partly to be spent helping others and being useful. At any rate, whether life is a test or not, tests are a part of life, especially in school, and how well you do on tests, as well as how hard you seem to be trying, can be pretty important to your parents and teachers. So do as well as you can.

It can help you and your parents to understand tests better, and thus to avoid puzzlement or friction, if you know some facts.

Intelligence tests are supposed to measure your intelligence. They give an "intelligence quotient," an IQ. Although they provide useful evidence, actually they are only a *score* on a series of questions. It's important to say, "His IQ *score* is . . . " rather than "His IQ is . . . " Intelligence is far too complex a matter to be accurately expressed by a number. But if a person has a high IQ score, it's evidence that he or she has the capacity to do well in accademic subjects.

However, a low IQ score doesn't mean that a person cannot do well. Some people just aren't able to perform well on tests even though they may perform very well in school and life. Or they may have kinds of intelligence that aren't measured by the test—artistic intelligence, personal intelligence, physical intelligence.

Aptitude tests are supposed to measure your aptitude—ability—to deal with words and with numbers. They are not tests of a given subject.

Achievement tests are supposed to show how much information and skill you have acquired in a given subject—how well you actually do in a subject rather than just your aptitude to do the subject.

Intelligence tests, aptitude tests, and achievement tests are published tests given in large numbers of schools. They are *standardized tests*. That means they compare your performance with established **standards**—with the performance of people in your city or state or nation. They also enable a school to compare the performance level of its students with that of students in other schools.

The results of many achievement tests are given in *percentiles* (50th percentile would be in the middle) or *grade equivalents* (8.3 would mean a performance level like that of an average student in the third month of eighth grade; 10.2 would be higher; 6.7 would be lower).

You may have noticed that I said that published tests are "supposed" to measure. Sometimes they do; sometimes they don't, so teachers, parents, and you should use them just as a part of the evidence, not as absolute truth.

In addition to published, standardized tests there are teacher-made (or sometimes school-made) tests, which are not standardized. They enable you to know how well you are doing in a course in a given subject. They range all the way from informal quizzes, to periodic major tests over a unit of material, to examinations, which give you a chance to show how well you have learned the information and skills taught in the course. In most quizzes, tests, and examinations, you are given a grade. Treat **grades** as information, not as some medal to be awarded or disgrace to be meted out. Be sure you understand what it means and what it tells you, and try to share this with your parents. (See also **report cards**.)

It will help you do well on teacher-made major tests and examinations if you review for them intelligently and take them intelligently. Doing well, if you can, is great for its own sake, and it certainly pleases parents and teachers. (See also **study habits**.)

Suggestions for reviewing. Assemble all the materials given to you during the course (books, worksheets, earlier tests), plus notes you have made. Look over all this material, but don't actually reread it. That is, look at the headings (if you recall nothing from the heading, then reread that part); notice underlined or italicized words, lists, etc.; look at exercises and study questions; memorize rules, formulas, and lists you're supposed to know. Look over your own notes, especially noticing things that the teacher stressed. If you have questions as you review, ask them in class during the review period, or after class. If you have lots of notes, make new shorter notes from them that summarize the key points. Try to figure out what sort of questions you would ask if you were the teacher and find out how to answer those. Sleep well the night before the test.

Suggestions for taking tests and exams. Get to the testing place early, all materials ready. Before you start actually writing on a major test, glance over all the questions just to see what's involved. If an idea flashes into your head, jot it down before you forget it. Plan your time so that each question gets its fair share. Leave some blank space at the end of each answer in case you have time to come back to it later and add more. Be sure to read all directions and questions *carefully,* so that you aren't writing on the wrong subject. Write legibly but not too slowly. Never waste time copying your answers. Just be sure all the words are clear. Unless you are required to answer the questions in order, do first those you know best, but don't spend more time than is allotted for the question.

Save maybe 5 percent of your time to reread and revise

your answers—that is, to proofread what you've written. If your style of taking exams is different from all this, and *if* it works well, ignore these suggestions. However, to avoid misunderstanding with parents and teachers, explain why you're doing so.

time together

It's obvious, I guess, that if you're to live well with people, you need to spend some time together talking, listening, communicating, enjoying things, working on problems, laughing, and maybe even crying (*see* **communication**). And yet many families get so busy with their own individual lives and work and pleasures that they don't really spend much time together, except maybe for eating meals as fast as possible, or perhaps sitting together drugged or dominated by TV (*see* **TV**). If finding time together is a problem in your family, I suggest that you make a point of saying sometime when the family will listen (or to your mother or father, to be passed on to others), "Look, I think we need to spend more time together, when we can just talk." (For suggestions about this *see* **talking things over.**) Or: "We seem to have all our fun apart. How about if we plan to [whatever it may be] *together*—maybe next Saturday?"

Family Council

Some families find it works well to agree in advance that every Saturday morning from 9:30 to 10:30 (or any other agreed-upon time), there will be a family council. At this meeting anyone can bring up any subject for discussion: practical problems, new ideas, strongly held feelings. It's understood that everyone in the family comes to the family meeting unless some unchangeable appointment or duty makes it impossible. If that is the case, they say so in advance.

You also may need some time together with your mother or your father. Tell her or him, say how important it is, and make a definite plan for it. Many parents would be wonderfully pleased to have you take the initiative in this, because they feel almost shy about imposing themselves on you and yet would love to have a chance to talk and listen.

Class Meeting
In school, obviously a class spends a lot of time together, but usually it has to do with teaching and learning the subject and skills of the course. Sometimes a feeling develops among students (or in the teacher) that it would be useful to spend some time not on the subject but on the life, problems, morale, or behavior of the class. If that's the case—and especially if there are problems like cheating, noisiness, lateness, rudeness, teasing, resentment, or feelings of being overworked—a useful device can be to schedule a class meeting. (For specific suggestions for how to proceed in a class meeting, see **conflicts**.) Of course, it doesn't always have to be about problems. It can be fun to have a class meeting just to share things the class is especially enjoying, or personal events that would help you all understand each other better and enjoy each other more.

Warning: Remember that the main purpose of school is learning, and most of the learning is and should be subjects and skills. If a class gets off too much into what some people call "touchy-feely stuff," it's not good education. But if there are problems or misunderstandings that are making it difficult to learn, using class meetings to get those matters out in the open and dealt with is well worth the time.

tone of voice
To live well with people it helps to listen carefully to their tone of voice, the way they say their words. A voice can be violent, soothing, friendly, repelling, attractive, depressing, cheering, careful, or just neutral. Think of the ways people say the word *really*: "Really?" "Really." "*Really*!" and so on. Try a few just for fun—maybe with your parents, letting

another person try to say what each "really" really does mean underneath the word. Try the same with "thanks," "let's go," "please," and "too bad," followed by the person's name. A little exercise like that is fun, and it makes everybody more aware of what they sound like—the messages they are getting across. The exercise can be useful and entertaining in school, too. And it's certainly useful to know what's behind your teachers' tone of voice at different times. "It's not what you say, but how you say it." (*See also* **language; moods; words.**)

Sometimes someone will say, "You sound angry," when you don't feel angry. It helps to try to hear your own voice. Tape your voice sometime, or tape a conversation, and hear how you sound. It's often a shock, because we don't hear our voices as others do. Also, it can be useful, if you're not angry but sound angry (or bored, or unfriendly, or whatever), to say, "But that's not how I feel. I'll have to listen better to myself."

transportation

Anything as important as getting from place to place in our complex lives is bound to lead to all sorts of misunderstanding and conflict unless teenagers and parents keep talking about it and working out plans so that everyone's important needs can be met safely. Basically, as long as you are living at home and your parents are responsible for your support and welfare, you have a duty to keep them informed about three things: where you are going, when, and how you will get there and back. And of course they have the responsibility for making it possible for you to get where you need to go and back, or of approving of the arrangements you make. Most of us no longer live in villages and near most of our friends and activities. We are a spread-out society.

The major source of concern about transportation in families is the car—the family's car or the cars of others. Cars, obviously, are both wonderful conveniences and very dangerous if not used competently and responsibly. Thus, if you are not yet old enough to get a driver's license, you should let your parents know who other than they will be driving you to various places, especially if the driver is a teenage friend of yours. Answer all your parents' questions about the people you drive with or, even better, provide them with information before they have to ask.

A vast step forward to independence is when you get a license and can drive yourself. Of course, passing the state driver's test is proof of a certain degree of competence, but it is reasonable for your parents to want to spend some time in the car with you at the wheel to be satisfied that you meet *their* standards of competence—not only mechanical competence and driving skill but also judgment. (I'm not suggesting that all teenage drivers are less competent and have poorer judgment than all adult drivers. You may become a better and safe driver than your parents. In fact, you may feel the need to suggest to one or both of your parents how they can be better drivers. If you do, make your suggestions tactfully!—but make them.)

If you have a license and are driving, offer to help pay for your share of the cost of gasoline and car maintenance. Perhaps this can come out of your **allowance** or your earnings. It might even help to make you responsible and your parents confident about your requests to use the car if they increased your allowance enough to allow for a reasonable amount of car use. The car and transportation are important enough matters to become a part of the agenda for family meetings from time to time. (*See* **time together**.)

Never, but never, drive a car when you are under the influence of **alcohol**. Also, do not accept a ride from a driver who has been drinking too much. It's much better to call home, or ask a friend or parent of a friend, for a ride. And be careful not to drive when you are very angry. **Anger** can ruin your judgment and make you do wild things. Wait. Calm down. Then drive.

TV

Television—whether to watch it, when to watch it, the effects of watching it, who controls it—is one of the major causes of friction between parents and children and between teachers and students. (A recent study showed that use of TV is also the second greatest cause of conflict between wives and husbands, the first being how best to spend the family's money.)

There's no doubt that TV is a valuable resource and can enrich our lives tremendously, both with information and entertainment. But there's no doubt, either, that it often stifles thought, interferes with homework, and dominates the lives of many families so that they don't really live well together but, rather, live side by side in front of the tube. TV can be addicting—it's been called "the plug-in drug." It's there, you turn it on, and it's terribly hard to turn off. Furthermore, while it's on, it can't be argued with. You can't make it pause while you consider, object, and think. It just bounds ahead, colorfully and powerfully. It gives vividly entertaining angles on life with the purpose of winning as high as possible a place on the rating scales. It's so lively that for many it makes the slow, steady pace of a classroom, or even of reading, seem dull. (Teachers can't change their color, bounce around, zoom in, and call down spaceships or supermonsters.) Its portrayal of family life is usually false, or at best distorted—not a very good basis for the realities of living together. One can understand why for twenty years now many people have called it "the boob tube."

However, whether we approve or not, TV is here to stay, so we need to learn how best to live with it and make it a strengthener of family life and schoolwork, and of relations between teenagers and their parents and teachers. This is urgent, for at present the average graduate from high school will, during his or her school years, have spent 11,000 hours in the classroom and 18,000 hours watching TV. Here are some suggestions.

TV at home. Spend some time talking together about what TV programs the family (or parts of it) will watch together. When you do watch a program with your parents, after it's over, no matter how great the temptation is to go on watching, turn off the TV and discuss the program.

What did you learn from it? What was entertaining about it? What faults did it have? In what senses was it true and in what senses false? If the program is to be continued next week, or tomorrow, should you all watch it again? (See also Sitcom Sessions under **talking things over**.) In other words, watch TV *critically,* using your brain.

Tastes do differ, there's no doubt about that. If there's a program that is very appealing to some members of the family and not to others, allow for that. People have a right to their own pleasures if they don't harm others (or themselves). If there's space, have a room in the house set aside for the TV so that it doesn't dominate the family living spaces. If the house is small, get earphones for the TV so that others will not be disturbed. If the family can afford it, maybe it's good to have more than one TV so that different needs can be met. However, your parents have a responsibility to help you see to it, if necessary, that access to your own TV is not interfering with your schoolwork or other parts of your life.

TV and school. Homework must come first—in importance if not necessarily in time. In fact, you can sometimes help yourself get through a long, hard school project by promising yourself a reward of a snack and half an hour of TV *after* two hours of solid work, or after completing a certain job. Suggest to teachers TV programs that you think would enrich the subject you are learning—perhaps a science program, a dramatization of a good book, a play, an analysis of a social problem you have been discussing. (Remember, many teachers work so hard they haven't time to keep up-to-date on what's really good on TV.) If a class is assigned to watch a TV program, try to make sure it gets discussed in class afterward. Remember that most TV situation programs show teachers in a false way, or as stereotyped people (tyrants, old maids, show-offs, strict bores, geniuses). Don't judge your teachers by TV stereotypes! It's all acting on TV.

typing see **study habits**

unfairness

People, whether they be teenagers, parents, or teachers, sometimes feel they aren't being treated fairly. They think, or even say or shout, "That's unfair!" We are all somewhat self-centered, and therefore when our self seems to be getting shoved or exploited, given too little or told to do too much, we feel unjustly treated. "That's unfair!"

If you feel that way about what your parents are doing, it's OK to say so now and then. It's a clearly received early-warning system. The same should go for when they say it to you. Either way, unless it's so obviously unfair that no more need be said (like being made to wash the dishes three nights in a row when the agreement had been to take turns), it's time to talk it over. Don't let a feeling of unfairness fester and grow in you till it gets to be resentment or even leads to **rebellion**.

Before you talk, however—maybe even before you say "That's unfair!"—it often helps to try to put yourself in the other person's situation. Looked at from their point of view, would the behavior seem unfair? And when you talk together, you both—as a sort of game—can try arguing it from the other's viewpoint. That can lead to understanding.

At school, if you think a teacher is treating you unfairly, don't just let it pass, unless it's a minor matter and happens only once or twice. Teachers have many, many students to deal with, and they're bound to make a few mistakes that look like unfairness. But if you really are sure you're being treated unfairly, try to figure out why. If there's something *you* can change to cure the situation, do it. If you can't figure out why, or if you can and the treatment *is* unfair, ask the teacher about it, preferably after class or some time when the teacher has a free moment to see you. Be sure you ask, not complain. Only if your asking doesn't bring an explanation and solution should you complain. Complaining—or **protesting**—should be a last resort.

If you don't get results and fairness out of all this, you may want to tell the school principal about the situation. Before you do this, it's better to let your teacher know that you're going to do it. It's also probably a good idea to talk it over with your parents. They may see a way out that you don't. Remember, no matter who you go to, you're still going to be taught by the teacher, so be careful not to create any deep bad feeling. Some of the kinds of unfairness that it's good to get straightened out are: marks on major papers or **report cards** that seem too low, given your performance; **punishment** for something you know you didn't do (*see* **honesty**); being put in a section or track of courses that seems to you not suited to your abilities and interests. Especially if you want a more challenging course or group than you've been admitted to, say so. But first get your facts together to try to prove it. Use facts, and your ambition, not just complaints. Get your parents in on this if it's really serious. (*See* **parent-teacher conferences.**)

Gripe Sharing

Agree in the family, or maybe with your teacher in class, to hold a sort of meeting when it's understood that the subject will be "What Gripes Me" or "Things That Bother Me." The rules are: You go around the group, in turn, each one speaking briefly about a gripe or bother. (Anyone who has nothing to say may pass.) Only after all have had a chance to speak do you discuss what has been said. Before you finish the session, go around the group again to be sure nothing important has been left unsaid. Agree in advance, though, on a time when the session will end. Gripes must be based on facts, not rumor, and no general accusations may be made, like, "Jack always [whatever]." Rather it should be, "When Jack [whatever]."

values

In discussing **peer pressure** I reported that 90 percent of the students I surveyed answered *yes* to the question, "Do you generally approve of the moral and social standards of your family?" This is a surprisingly high percentage of approval, because we so often hear about differences, quarreling, and friction between parents and teenagers on those matters.

It is useful and interesting for parents, teachers, and teenagers to discuss some of their deeply held moral values, or to discuss values that are puzzling, not deeply held, or even opposed. Under the topic **sex** I listed eight values: the infinite worth of each person, consideration, communication, family, responsibility, pleasure and good feelings, control, and information. You might want to look again at the fuller explanation of them, for they can be applied to all aspects of life, not just sex. And you'll find that an excellent way to develop understanding between yourself and your parents and teachers is to discuss these values, or another set of values you may want to write out for yourself.

words

Exchange of words is one of the main ways we get along with each other. Obviously, therefore, it helps you in **communication** with others if you know lots of words and how to use them. Here are some suggestions.

If you don't understand a word somebody uses, politely stop them and say, "What was that word? I don't know what it means." It's much better to do that than to let it pass, and certainly most teachers will take it as a sign of alertness and intelligence if you ask. If you learn a new word, it can be quite interesting to use it, say, at home, just to get a little discussion going. You might ask, "Dad, was that comment of yours meant to be pejorative?" If Dad knows that *pejorative* means *belittling* or a *put-down*, he'll be pleased that you know too. If he doesn't, you can have the satisfaction of saying what it means, and that should be pleasing to both of you.

Words aren't, in themselves, good or bad. They are just words. But words get feelings attached to them, and they can shock and antagonize people. In a school classroom, it's almost always best to use standard, proper words, carefully and accurately. Linguistically, the classroom and the locker room are quite different places—so "Watch your

work load

There used to be a saying: "People who have half an hour to spend always spend it with somebody who hasn't." Well, parents and teachers—and you—have quite a lot of work to do, and it's often wise, before you ask somebody to listen or to do something, to start with "Have you got time?" or "Are you in a rush?" or "How's your work load, because I can ask this later?"

Furthermore, it's a good idea for you to keep those you live with informed about your own work load: "I'm going to be pretty busy with exams [or rehearsals, or sports practice, or whatever] for the next few days, so try to understand if I'm not my usual helpful self," or something like that.

On the opposite side, if things ease up, say, "Well, life's a little better for a few days now, so if you want me to [whatever], this would be a good time."

Keep tuned, and try to give others evidence so they can keep tuned.

yelling

Yelling is a sort of voice tool, used to get things done or to destroy. It's a great way to cheer people on or warn them of danger. Are there any other good reasons to yell? It does get you heard—but perhaps not listened to—and it shows that you feel strongly about something. It can clear the air and make you feel better, provided it doesn't make other people feel worse. In some families it is an accepted form of communication; one may hear a good bit of yelling, parent to child, child to parent, and yet often there's also lots of hugging and sharing.

However, yelling is usually a substitute for thinking. It often arises from anger, arouses anger in the person yelled at, and gets out of control, so that you say or do things that really hurt. If it becomes a habit, it may carry over into situations where it gets you into bad trouble.

Too much yelling annoys other people, inside and outside the family. If your family does a lot of yelling, **talking things over** is probably a good idea. Find out how each person's yelling affects the others, and discuss ways of stopping to think before raising your voice.

Yelling in class is an affront to most teachers. It makes them feel out of control and not respected, and it sounds bad. If, on the other hand, you have teachers who yell at you or the class and you find it hard to take, find a time to say so quietly and describe how it makes you feel. These teachers may not be aware of how much they are yelling.

your room/locker/desk

At home, unless you say you don't want it, you have a right to **privacy**, to your own private place, where you can go and do and think what you want as long as you are not disturbing anyone else. If your house is crowded and there isn't a room for you alone, at least you should have your own private screened-off space within a shared room. At school, you have a right to your own locker or homeroom desk, yours to use as you want, not subject to inspection, again provided you aren't disturbing anyone. (Keeping smelly old socks in your locker will disturb others. Your rights must be enjoyed with consideration.)

Back to the subject of your room for a moment. If you have a mother or a father with deeply felt **standards** about order, neatness, and cleanliness in the house, it will be disturbing to them to know that behind the closed door of your room is a chaos of unmade bed and junk all over the place, even though you yourself are able to live happily within it. Consideration for your parents' feelings requires you, therefore, to keep your room in a state that won't be a source of anguish to others. "That awful mess in there!" they may think, and be unhappy about it. Thus, it's a good plan to discuss your room and its condition, to invite your parents in now and then, and to work out an agreement that will satisfy you and them. Also, if your room is such a mess that you can't find things and live efficiently within it, so that you can play your part in the life of the family, things need changing, and it's your responsibility to change them. As one parent said, "I told her to keep her room neat or else make an environmental impact statement."

Somewhat the same thing goes for your desk or locker. If you can do your school tasks efficiently or on time from a locker that many people would consider a mess, OK. But if rummaging around in it causes you to clutter up the hall or room, causes you not to be able to find what you need, or makes you late to classes, then you need help, and your teachers or hall-duty people have a right to inspect your premises. But they should talk with you about it first and arrange for the inspection when you are present.

you yourself

Ending a book with an item like the last one, which includes smelly socks and the disturbing effects of sloppiness, doesn't seem quite right. It's too small, if not too smelly, a subject. Let's end with *you*.

Remember, you are unique, one of a kind. Remember the equation in the introduction that expresses this uniqueness: *your unique heredity + your unique environment = unique you*: YUH + YUE = UY. It sounds almost like a mysterious religious chant, doesn't it? But it's true!

In order to live well with your parents and teachers you need to work out ways to be your unique self—but still, of course, relating with others. This means you must recognize that your parents and your teachers also are unique. And thus, with our uniquenesses in common, both valued and respected, we can enjoy and strengthen and enrich each other—most of the time. It's not easy, but nothing is more worth the effort. In essence, that's how to live with parents and teachers.

Bibliography

Calderone, Mary, and Eric Johnson. *The Family Book About Sexuality.* New York: Harper & Row, 1981; Bantam Books, 1983.

Getzoff, Ann, and Carolyn McClenahan. *Stepkids: A Survival Guide for Teenagers in Stepfamilies.* New York: Walker & Co.,1984.

Gilligan, Carol. *In a Different Voice: Psychological Theory and Woman's Development.* Boston: Harvard University Press, 1982.

Johnson, Corinne Benson, and Eric Johnson. *Love and Sex and Growing Up.* New York: Bantam Books, 1979.

Johnson, Eric. *How to Achieve Competence in English: A Quick Reference Handbook.* New York: Bantam Books, 1979.

——. *How to Live Through Junior High School*, new ed. Philadelphia: J. B. Lippincott Co., 1975.

——. *Love and Sex in Plain Language*, 4th ed. New York: Harper & Row, 1985; Bantam Books, 1985.

——. *People, Love, Sex, and Families.* New York: Walker & Co., 1985.

——. *Raising Children to Achieve.* New York: Walker & Co., 1984.

——. *Sex: Telling It Straight.* Philadelphia: J. B. Lippincott Co., 1970; Bantam Books, 1971.

——. *You Are the Editor.* Belmont, Calif.: Pitman Learning, 1981.

—— and David McClelland. *Learning to Achieve.* Glenview, Ill.: Scott, Foresman & Co., 1984.

Schowalter, John E., and Walter R. Anyan. *The Family Book of Adolescence: A Comprehensive Medically Oriented Guide to the Years from Puberty to Adulthood.* New York: Alfred A. Knopf, 1979.

Weil, Andrew, and Winifred Rosen. *Chocolate to Morphine: Understanding Mind-Active Drugs.* Boston: Houghton Mifflin Co., 1983.

Winship, Elizabeth C. *Reaching Your Teenager.* Boston: Houghton Mifflin Co., 1983.

Index of Games and Activities

Argue the Other Side	24	Mood Warnings	82
Class Meeting	141	Pantomimes	26–27
Conflict Resolution	35–36	Sentence Completion	50
Crime and Punishment	101–102	Sitcom Sessions	132
		Strength-O-Grams	97
"Dear Abby"	33	Switch Off and Listen	74
Family Checkbook	80	Topic Talking	133
Family Council	140	Trade-lasts	97
Gripe Sharing	147	Treat Yourself	117–118
The Hate Game	61	Unselfish Acts	117
His-and-Her Adjectives	124	"We Need to Talk About . . ."	132
Listen and Recap	74		
Making Faces	50–51	"What Makes Me Angry"	20
Making Up Rules	112–113	"Why I Would Like . . ."	118

Index of Subjects
(See also Contents)

abnormality, 84–85
acne, 23
addiction, 16, 46, 63, 125, 144
advice, 8, 16, 58, 63, 78, 104, 106
alcoholism, 16, 18, 47
appreciation, 62, 63, 96, 102, 106, 109, 116
authority, 21, 24, 53, 87, 104

books, 12, 27, 113
borrowing, 77, 79, 112
budgeting, 79
bullying, 35

cars and driving, 16, 28, 39, 92, 132, 142–143
chaperons, 90, 92
clothes, 22, 32, 35–36, 79, 95, 112
communication, 12, 19, 23, 43, 62, 63, 71–72, 100, 114, 121–122, 131–133, 140, 148, 149
competition, 10, 56
complaining, 34, 37, 57, 58, 100, 102, 103, 147
confidentiality, 64, 81, 89, 114–115, 136
conflict resolution, 35–36
conflicts, 10, 39, 41
consideration, 13, 71, 121, 127, 150

crashing, 89, 90, 108
criticism, 43
curfew, 38, 65

depression, 40, 63
drinking, 16–18, 39, 46, 89, 91, 93, 112, 143
dying, 40–41, 47

escape, 48, 98, 113
examinations, 48, 139
excuses, 26, 31, 48, 129

failure, 63
friction, 52, 89, 127, 135, 144, 148
fun, 8, 33, 45, 51, 54, 58, 110, 135, 140

going steady, 38–39, 57, 120
goofing off, 51, 55, 57, 93, 110
gossip, 107
grief, 16, 40, 59
guidance, 59, 60, 63

hitting, 19, 35, 51, 64, 66, 109
homework, 62–63, 64, 83, 84, 87, 107, 109, 117, 127–130, 144, 145
hostility, 44, 60, 98, 104, 105
hotlines, 30, 114, 131
humor, sense of, 105, 118

independence, 9, 10, 15, 70, 83, 87, 108, 143

Index of Subjects

IQ score, 69, 137–138
joking, 71

lateness, 77, 141, 151
laughter, 8, 29, 32, 47, 67, 72, 77
limits, 9, 22, 66, 72, 91, 110
lying, 32, 76, 98

male-female behavior, 76
marks, 78, 147
masturbation, 60, 120
motivation, 55, 56, 82

nagging, 37, 71, 80, 84, 125
neatness, 22–23, 77, 150
needs, 8–9, 10, 19, 46, 52, 74, 78, 83, 94, 116, 121, 142
noisiness, 77, 83, 112, 141

obedience, 83, 87, 102, 112
objectivity, 16, 59
obstacles, 56, 85

pantomimes, 26–27
parties, 17–18, 95, 106, 108
peers, 15, 92–93, 120, 126, 134
petting, 120
physical abuse, 29, 113
plagiarism, 28, 101, 112
politeness, 12, 76, 94
possessions, 34, 77
pregnancy, 15, 40, 54, 108, 120, 126
privacy, 9, 40, 47–48, 54, 86, 97, 110, 111, 114, 120, 131, 150
psychiatrist, 59, 64, 100, 131
psychological abuse, 29, 113
psychologist, 59, 63–64, 100

references, 70, 107

resentment, 27, 32, 36, 116, 141, 146
respect, 8, 12, 22, 29, 76, 95, 105, 110, 111, 114, 123, 134, 135, 150, 151
ridiculing, 32, 71, 105
room, 110, 150–151
rudeness, 141
rumors, 54, 107, 122, 147

self-control, 137
self-criticism, 36–37
self-discipline, 41–42, 63
self-punishment, 59
self-respect, 8, 121, 126
self-righteousness, 68
sex education, 120–121
sexual abuse, 29, 68, 69, 113
sleep, 8, 40, 61, 66, 109
sloppiness, 22, 31, 47, 150
stealing, 107, 112, 113, 115, 127
stepparents, 42–43, 44, 127
sulking, 32, 86
swearing, 131

talebearing, 65, 133
teetotaler, 47
telephoning, 54, 77
television, 52, 77, 137, 140, 143–145
tensions, 51, 66, 104
truancy, 63, 113
typing, 129–130, 145

uniqueness, 9–10, 151

white noise, 83
worthlessness, sense of, 63
wrongdoing, 25–26, 59, 64–65, 100–101, 134

www.ingramcontent.com/pod-product-compliance
Lightning Source LLC
Chambersburg PA
CBHW031251290426
44109CB00012B/535